Rational Behavior Therapy Center

Especially For

_____

Best Wishes
from

Maxie Maultsby

A MILLION DOLLARS FOR YOUR HANGOVER

THE ILLUSTRATED GUIDE
FOR THE NEW SELF-HELP
ALCOHOLIC TREATMENT METHOD

By Maxie C. Maultsby, Jr., M.D.

Illustrations by Hank Chapman

RATIONAL SELF-HELP BOOKS
Lexington, Kentucky

Other books by Dr. Maultsby:

Help Yourself To Happiness
You and Your Emotions
Emotional Well Being
Handbook of Rational Self-Counseling

Library of Congress Cataloging in Publication Data

Maultsby, Maxie C.
A million dollars for your hangover

Bibliography: p.
Includes index.
1. Alcoholism.   I. Title.
RC565.M34   616.8'61   78-27736
ISBN 0-932838-00-6

Copyright© 1978 by Maxie C. Maultsby, Jr.
Library of Congress Card Number
ISBN 0-932838-00-6
Published by Rational Self-Help Books
Division of R.S.A. Inc., 2036 Blairmore Rd.
Lexington, Ky. 40502

TABLE OF CONTENTS

INTRODUCTION .1
    Subtitles— AA is one way; Why a new self-help method?; What's new about the new treatment method?; Research on the New self-help method; About this book; Who can benefit from this book?; The three sections in this book; Aids to rapid learning; How to read this book; References; Emphasis questions and answers

    Section I 9a

Chapter 1 TYPES OF ALCOHOL DRINKING AND DRINKERS 10
    Subtitles— Why problem drinkers habitually abuse alcohol; Is a drinking problem an accident?; First clinical case history; Night caps for the lonely; Alcohol for sleep; Second clinical case history; Alcohol to wash away anger; The human brain works like a camera; Force versus choice; The Rebel-without-a-cause syndrome; History of an adolescent problem drinker; Alcohol to fit in with the crowd; What it means to be shy; Two important questions; Emphasis questions and answers

Chapter 2 THE PROCESS OF ALCOHOL ADDICTION. . . . 27
    Subtitles— Stop and go signs for alcohol drinkers; Behavioral Research Shows; Stage one of habitual problem drinking; Stage two of habitual problem drinking; Internal balance and physical well being; Alcohol is an addictive drug; Why the easy way gets hard; Those animals can frighten alcoholics to death; Four insights worth repeating; Alcohol to function; Alcohol to pay bills;

Alcohol to make life worth living; Alcohol to make the brain work better; Postponing problem drinking doesn't stop it; Why abstinence alone is not enough; The problem drinker's blind spot; What problem drinkers need; Rational Self-Counseling (RSC); Who's appropriate for RSC?; Emphasis questions and answers

Chapter 3 RATIONAL SELF-COUNSELING FOR
　　　　　　PROBLEM DRINKERS 43
　　Subtitles—　A common Question; What is Rational Self-Counseling?; When is self-counseling rational?; The five rules for Rational Self-Counseling; When is self-counseling irrational?; Psychosomatic facts supporting Rational Self-Counseling; Rational Self-Analysis and Rational Emotive Imagery; Why Rational Self-Counseling is ideal for problem drinkers; Emphasis questions and answers

Section II (part one) 49a

Chapter 4 THE ABC'S OF ALCOHOLIC SELF-HELP 50
　　Subtitles—　The emotional ABC's; Psychosomatic Fact #1; Emotional Insight #1; Psychosomatic Fact #2; Emotional Insight #2; The ABC's of your new negative emotions; Psychosomatic Fact #3; Psychosomatic Fact #4; Emphasis questions and answers

Chapter 5 ARE YOUR EMOTIONS REALLY AS SIMPLE
　　　　　　AS ABC? 61
　　Subtitles—　Psychosomatic Fact #5; Your Emotional ABC's; Emphasis questions and answers

Chapter 6 WHY THINKING IS MORE IMPORTANT THAN
　　　　　　EMOTIONAL FEELINGS 70
　　Subtitles—　The common mistake problem drinkers

make; What a healthy brain does and doesn't guarantee; Why people mistrust their thoughts; It's foolish to blindly trust your emotional feelings; Useful insights into gut thinking; Emphasis questions and answers

Chapter 7 THE RATIONAL USE OF YOUR EMOTIONAL ABC's 80
Subtitles— What your emotions do; What about acting against your emotions?; Are negative emotions healthy reactions?; How much, can be much more important than what type; Mentally and emotionally healthy behaviors; What is Rational Thinking?; Rational Rule #1; Rational Insight #1; Rational Rule #2; Rational Insight #2; Rational Rule #3; Rational Rule #4; Rational Rule #5; Rational Insight #3; The five rules for rational thinking; Can people really control themselves that rationally?; The five questions for rational thinking; Emphasis questions and answers

Chapter 8 WANTING VERSUS CRAVING A DRINK 95
Subtitles— Primary craving and drinking; Why most alcoholics usually choose alcohol; Secondary craving and jumping off the wagon; The myth of dry DT's; Wishes and wants; Hopes and desires; The rational view of needs; A four point summary; A common question; Table of learned and nonlearned urges to drink; Secondary craves; Nonlearned urges; Emphasis questions and answers

Chapter 9 TEACHING CURED ALCOHOLICS ABOUT ALCOHOL ADDICTION AND DE-ADDICTION . . 108
Subtitles— Use of the tape recorder in RSC; Self-disclosure in RSC; The process of de-addiction; You learn only in your brain; Emphasis questions and answers

Section II (part two) 121a

Chapter 10 THE ABC's OF RATIONAL SELF-ANALYSIS . . 122
  Subtitles— How to do an RSA; A well done RSA;
    Emphasis questions and answers

Chapter 11 RATIONAL EMOTIVE IMAGERY 138
  Subtitles— Haste usually makes the least speed; The
    instant calming maneuver (ICM); Old habits
    don't disappear just because you don't want
    them anymore; Daily recommended REI
    routine; REI on related events; Emphasis
    questions and answers

Chapter 12 USING RSA's FOR TREATMENT 147
  Subtitles— How to do therapy with RSA's; The RSA
    sequence in therapy; Bob's first RSA as
    therapy; A common mistake to avoid;
    Don't get confused there; Emphasis
    questions and answers

**Chapter 13 WHY YOUR ATTITUDE IS THE "IT" THAT
    UPSETS YOU** 157
  Subtitles— But facts don't control emotions; Why
    admitting to bad attitudes is not enough;
    Irrational should's trigger irrational anger;
    Helpful insights are for the patients;
    Rational shoulds are just good English; The
    power of rational thinking; Rational should's
    and science; Advice for beginning counselors;
    The value of systematic repetition; RSA's
    are not absolutely necessary; What if
    patients still don't progress?; Emphasis
    questions and answers

**Chapter 14 FROM DRINKING TO NONDRINKING
    BEHAVIOR** 172
  Subtitles— Science and human nature; Behavioral
    re-education; The wisdom of nature;
    Teaching patients about habit re-education;

Daily nondrinking practice; Emphasis questions and answers

Section III 181a

Chapter 15 THE INTENSIVE NEW SELF-HELP ALCOHOLIC TREATMENT PROGRAM 182
Subtitles— Schedule for the First Week; Correcting the special breed myth; Overnight assignment; Tuesday; Wednesday; Thursday; Friday; Weekend assignment; Sample schedule for the second week; Daily home-life plan; Follow-up care; Return to drinking; We admit the obvious; Social drinking is not for every problem drinker; Many could, but few will

Chapter 16 NONDRINKING TAPE SCRIPTS 196
Subtitles— Our standard, nondrinking, recorded lecture; Uniquely personal nondrinking scripts; Dr. Ryan's nondrinking script; Dr. Ryan's script continued; Was that brain-washing?; Emphasis questions and answers

Chapter 17 SUBTLE HABITS THAT MAINTAIN PROBLEM DRINKING 209
Subtitles— Acting out emotional white lies; Bob's reaction was normal but irrational; Proving the obvious; Calling the easiest act the hardest; Being afraid of alcohol; Emphasis questions and answers

Chapter 18 RATIONAL SELF-COUNSELING TO PREVENT ALCOHOL ABUSE 216
Subtitles— Conclusions; Summary

YIPE Test 224
References 228
Index 233

PROFESSIONAL ACKNOWLEDGMENT

I freely acknowledge my professional debt to the many clinical and research scientists whose past work made my work and this book possible. I could not and therefore have not tried to refer to them all. But I would like to acknowledge my special professional debt to Albert Ellis, Ph.D., creator of Rational Emotive Therapy from which I derived Rational Behavior Therapy and Rational Self-Counseling. I can sincerely say that without the early training I received from Dr. Ellis this book would not have been possible.

Introduction

There are more than 13 million American alcoholics. Each year another 200,000 alcohol drinkers become alcoholics. Another 50 to 60 million American lives are harmfully influenced by those alcoholics. The yearly cost to the American economy of its alcoholics is between 10 and 15 billion dollars. Those facts make alcoholism one of the most common and costly American social health problems.

Habitual alcohol abuse causes alcoholism, but the following three-step medical treatment quickly cures it.

STEP ONE
STOP ALCOHOLIC DRINKING

That can be quite dangerous. Without medical care, up to 25 percent of advanced alcoholics will die if they suddenly stop drinking. For them the hospital is the safest place to take step one.

STEP TWO
MEDICALLY TREAT ALCOHOL WITHDRAWAL

STEP THREE
MEDICALLY TREAT THE ALCOHOL-INDUCED ILLNESSES

A few of the serious alcohol induced illnesses alcoholics often have are: gastritis, liver damage, anemia, malnutrition and pneumonia. Except for those problems, however, within less than three weeks of good medical care most alcoholics will dry out and be cured. BUT! There's a BIG CATCH-22: CURING ALCOHOLISM DOES NOT STOP HABITUAL ALCOHOL ABUSE: **it just delays it.** That's why **within a year** of treatment **most cured (dry) alcoholics** take a running:

JUMP OFF THE WAGON

THAT'S RIGHT! Alcoholics don't fall off the wagon; they take a running jump. Why? Mainly for two reasons:
1. They are confused about what their main problem is.
2. Their treatment hasn't taught them how to live happily without alcohol.

Unfortunately most alcoholics mistakenly believe their main problem is alcoholism. That's why it's common to hear them say:

"Doc, this is the fifth time I've been treated. So this time I want you-all to keep me as long as it takes to really cure me. Give me a triple dose if that's what it takes. I'm really tired of this disease. I don't ever want to have alcoholism again."

Such alcoholics are confused. **Their main problem is not alcoholism.** Their main problem is habitual alcohol abuse, most accurately called HABITUAL PROBLEM DRINKING—that is, drinking to solve personal problems. For such alcoholics to stay cured, they must learn how to solve their personal problems without alcohol.

AA IS ONE WAY

For over forty years, AA (Alcoholics Anonymous) has been proving what recent research clearly shows: problem drinkers can be taught how to stop habitual problem drinking. But if they stop, they have to do it themselves. All that friends, relatives, physicians, psychotherapists, or counselors can do is teach problem drinkers what they need to know to stop drinking. And over **a half million dollars in recent research** indicates that the NEW SELF-HELP ALCOHOLIC TREATMENT METHOD is as effective as AA in teaching alcoholics to stop problem drinking.

WHY A NEW SELF-HELP METHOD IS NEEDED

Almost twice as many alcoholics get treatment from AA than from medical and other health professionals. Yet, most research studies show that AA **does not give any more effective treatment to alcoholics than health professionals give.** That fact indicates that alcoholics prefer self-help treatment methods to those of traditional health professionals. BUT, **less than 10 percent of America's 10 million alcoholics** accept AA's self-help treatment. Consequently, over 85% of America's alcoholics are not receiving any treatment. Obviously, therefore, we need other types of self-help treatment methods that are as effective as AA. That's why I recommend the NEW SELF-HELP ALCOHOL TREATMENT METHOD.

WHAT'S NEW ABOUT THE NEW SELF-HELP TREATMENT METHOD?

First, its self-help techniques are based on a research-tested psychosomatic learning theory of human behavior.

Second, its self-help techniques were developed from clinical research on teaching people how to help themselves without drugs.

Third, its self-help techniques are easy for both professionals and lay people to learn and to teach to alcoholics.

Fourth, its self-help techniques are easy for habitual problem drinkers to teach to themselves.

Fifth, its self-help techniques are routinely used by health professionals who practice Rational Behavior Therapy* as opposed to only traditional psychotherapy.

Sixth, the families of habitual problem drinkers can quickly learn to use these self-help techniques to help themselves and their alcoholic loved ones to stabilize their relationships and strengthen their family unity.

Seventh, the NEW SELF-HELP ALCOHOLIC TREATMENT METHOD teaches habitual problem drinkers how to solve their personal problems with improved thinking instead of problem drinking.

Eighth, the NEW SELF-HELP ALCOHOLIC TREATMENT METHOD enables habitual problem drinkers to rely on themselves (rather than on outside groups) to solve their drinking problems.

RESEARCH ON THE NEW SELF-HELP METHOD

In 1972 my associates (Dr. Jeffrey Brandsma and Mr. Richard Welsh) and I received a four-year research grant** to evaluate Rational Self-Counseling or RSC, as a new self-help alcoholic treatment method. Our four out-patient alcoholic treatment groups were:

1. A Rational Self-Counseling treatment group taught by a lay-person who had learned RSC by receiving it as self-help treatment for his own personal problems.
2. An Alcoholics Anonymous treatment group, run by AA counselors selected by the local AA organization.
3. A traditional Insight Psychotherapy treatment group conducted by professional Insight Psychotherapists.
4. A Rational Behavior Therapy treatment group conducted by professional Rational Behavior Therapists.***

Our research indicated that Rational Self-Counseling (taught either by professionally trained counselors and therapists or by our

---

*Rational Behavior Therapy (formulated by Maxie C. Maultsby, Jr., M.D.) is an extension of Rational Emotive Therapy, formulated by Albert Ellis, Ph.D.

**Research Grant #R01-AA00496-04 from the National Institute on Alcohol Abuse and Alcoholism, Dept. of Health, Education and Welfare.

***There was also a fifth, no-treatment control group.

lay-counselors) was as effective as treatment by Alcoholics Anonymous.*

ABOUT THIS BOOK

In the fall of 1977 I received a grant from the Bureau of Health Resources (in the Department of Health, Education and Welfare) to design an intensive five-day training course to teach physicians, psychotherapists, health administrators, educators, and professional and lay alcohol counselors from Federal Region IV, how to treat problem drinkers with the New Self-Help Alcoholic Treatment Method. An improved version of that intensive five-day training course in the NEW SELF-HELP ALCOHOLIC TREATMENT METHOD is now offered to all interested health professionals and to working lay alcohol counselors several times per year at the Training Center for Rational Behavior Therapy and Emotional Self-Help, University of Kentucky Medical College, Lexington, Kentucky 40506.

Based on my experiences as the director of the above research and training programs, I developed this illustrated case history guide for learning and teaching The NEW SELF-HELP ALCOHOLIC TREATMENT METHOD.

WHO CAN BENEFIT FROM THIS BOOK?

1. PROBLEM DRINKERS, motivated to solve their personal problem by themselves.
2. ANYONE who thinks his or her frequent alcohol abuse might really be habitual problem drinking.
3. PHYSICIANS, PSYCHOTHERAPISTS, COUNSELORS AND TRAINED LAY-PEOPLE who want to teach problem drinkers how to help themselves without alcohol.
4. All undergraduate and graduate STUDENTS in the MENTAL HEALTH or OTHER HEALTH fields.

---

*Treatment by professional Insight Therapists was similarly effective.

5. EDUCATORS who want to use the classroom to help prevent alcohol abuse by adolescents and adults.
6. INTELLIGENT PEOPLE who want to be informed about the NEWEST SELF-HELP TREATMENT METHOD for one of society's major health problems.

THE THREE SECTIONS IN THIS BOOK

Section ONE describes the FACTS AND INSIGHTS needed for the most useful understanding of problem drinking and alcoholism.

Section TWO uses step-by-step instructions for learning and teaching the emotional and behavioral self-help techniques used in the NEW SELF-HELP ALCOHOLIC TREATMENT METHOD.

Section THREE describes our Intensive Self-Help Alcoholic Treatment Program and research indicating that courses in RATIONAL SELF-COUNSELING taught in public schools have great potential as economical, yet practical and effective means of decreasing the currently growing numbers of problem drinkers and alcoholics in American school populations.

Each section uses frequent illustrations, typical case history material, and the everyday language of intelligent lay people to make learning fast and easy.

AIDS TO RAPID LEARNING

After each chapter there is a list of emphasis questions, prepared by Ms. Susan Gaffield, M.S., and Ms. Linda Carpenter, M.S., training coordinators on my staff at the Training Center for Rational Behavior Therapy and Emotional Self-Help. These emphasis questions reinforce the most important facts and insights you will have just covered. So answer each of them.

If the answers seem easy, that will prove you have learned the most useful facts in the chapter. But if you miss three or more questions from any one group, you will benefit most by re-reading that chapter immediately.

The correct answers to the emphasis questions appear at the end of each chapter. But resist the urge to peek; write your answers before you look at the correct ones.

HOW TO READ THIS BOOK

RAPIDLY at first; it's a skimmer's delight. You can skim this book within an hour. Just read the SUBTITLES, BOLD TYPE and ILLUSTRATIONS. Then re-read everything more slowly.

This is a SELF-INSTRUCTIONAL, SELF-HELP book. Such books teach you best if you read them **rapidly, then more slowly, and then still more slowly and thoughtfully.**

REFERENCES

This book is a practical guide for busy health professionals, paraprofessionals, educators, and intelligent lay people. That's why it's **not cluttered with references.** But Dr. Mary Greene (Intensive Treatment Coordinator on my staff) has listed at the end of the book the most important references for each section. Those references, plus the ones they list, will probably satisfy even the most research-minded reader.

EMPHASIS QUESTIONS

1. _____ alcohol _____ causes alcoholism.
2. The _____ step medical _____ method _____ alcoholism.
3. Having their alcoholism cured is all alcoholics need to solve their drinking problem. True or False?
4. Within a _____ most cured (dry) alcoholics take a _____ _____ off the _____.
5. Alcoholics fall off the wagon. True or False?
6. The main problem of alcoholics is _____ alcohol _____ known as _____ problem _____.
7. To help alcoholics stay cured, you must teach them how to

solve their _____ problems without _____.
8. Alcoholics Anonymous is a very effective way to treat some alcoholics. True or False?
9. We need new treatment methods for those alcoholics who seem inappropriate for AA. True or False?
10. There are _____ new things about THE NEW ALCOHOLIC SELF-HELP TREATMENT METHOD.
11. Name those eight new things referred to in question 10 above.
12. A half million dollars worth of scientific research supports THE NEW SELF-HELP ALCOHOLIC TREATMENT METHOD. True or False?
13. The Department of Health, Education and Welfare has funded training programs to teach practicing alcoholic counselors the NEW SELF-HELP ALCOHOLIC TREATMENT METHOD. True or False?
14. This case history guide for teaching and learning the NEW SELF-HELP ALCOHOLIC TREATMENT METHOD was based on the _____ and training programs formulated by the author and funded by HEW grants.
15. At least six groups of people can benefit from reading this book. Name them.
16. This book is meant to entertain you. True or False?
17. This is a _____ INSTRUCTION, SELF _____ book that needs to be read _____ at first, then more _____ then more slowly and _____.

CORRECT ANSWERS

1. Habitual, abuse
2. three, treatment, cures
3. False
4. year, running, jump, wagon
5. False
6. habitual, abuse, habitual, drinking
7. personal, alcohol
8. True
9. True
10. eight
11. (see page 4)
12. True
13. True
14. research
15. (see page 6 for answer)
16. False
17. SELF, HELP, rapidly, slowly, thoughtfully

SECTION I

"It's a mystery to me; I just don't understand why they keep on drinking." That's one of the most common comments health professionals as well as lay people make about problem drinkers. Yet those confused people most often are the ones who try to get habitual problem drinkers to stop drinking. That's probably one of the main reasons more than 85 percent of America's problem drinkers refuse to accept any form of treatment.

The following chapters describe the basic facts and insights needed to understand habitual problem drinking. They also explain why Rational Self-Counseling is an ideal self-help technique for problem drinkers:

Chapter 1 Types of Alcohol Drinking and Drinkers

Chapter 2 The Process of Alcohol Addiction

Chapter 3 Rational Self-Counseling for Problem Drinkers

Before you read a chapter, read each subtitle and change it to the topic of a question. For example: Change *Why Problem Drinkers Habitually Abuse Alcohol* to: "Yes, Why do problem drinkers habitually abuse alcohol?" Now you are most likely to look for and find the answer when you read Chapter 1. You are also most likely to remember that answer and put it to use.

1

Types of Alcohol Drinking and Drinkers

Almost all Americans drink some alcohol—at least an occasional beer or glass of wine—just to be friendly. That's **sociable** drinking by SOCIABLE DRINKERS.

Well over half the American population drinks alcohol regularly for its pleasant taste and other refreshing features. That's social drinking by SOCIAL DRINKERS.

Then there are the **more than ten million Americans who habitually** drink alcohol to cope better with their problems in daily living. Unfortunately though, such drinking usually creates many more problems than it solves. That's problem drinking by PROBLEM DRINKERS.

WHY PROBLEM DRINKERS HABITUALLY ABUSE ALCOHOL

Usually, for the same basic reasons you and I (and most people) habitually do the things we do: Because of PERSONAL HOPES AND/OR FEARS. Those two basic motivational urges explain most voluntarily repeated behavior by normal people. Unfortunately, when the repeated behavior is frequent alcohol abuse, **a drinking problem usually is an accidental, but unavoidable result.**

IS A DRINKING PROBLEM AN ACCIDENT?

YES, in most cases. Problem drinkers almost never intend to create their drinking problems. But because alcohol is an addictive drug, if anyone abuses it enough, he or she will create a drinking problem, without ever intending or desiring to do so.

TO MAKE USEFUL INSIGHTS ABOUT PROBLEM DRINKERS

1. Remember, their drinking problems are unavoidable accidents, resulting from sincere, but inappropriate reactions to personal hopes and fears.

2. When problem drinkers describe their drinking habits, look for what they have been hoping to get by drinking alcohol, and/or what they have been afraid of getting if they don't drink it.

3. **Don't confuse TRUTH with FACT.** The two are often opposites. FACTS are what exist whether people know about them or not, like them or not, or believe or admit to them or not. TRUTH is merely a personal belief; it exists only in a person's mind. **That's why truth may not and often does not describe facts.**

Fortunately, American courts of law accept and act on those facts about facts. The courts know that even an eyewitness to a crime may not know what the facts were. That's why **American courts never require witnesses to swear to the FACTS, the whole FACTS and nothing but the FACTS.** Witnesses in American courts are only required to swear to the TRUTH, the whole TRUTH and nothing but the TRUTH.

American courts know that truth is merely a personal belief. Legally competent people usually know what they believe. When their beliefs can aid the courts in the pursuit of justice, it's reasonable for the courts to require those people to describe their beliefs. That's why the courts do it.

4. When problem drinkers say they want to stop drinking, assume they are telling the truth. They usually are, at least at the moment they say it. But if you have good reason to believe they are lying, then simply point out that if they are lying, they are playing a vicious little game in which no one can win and they will ultimately lose the most.

Many of the beliefs problem drinkers have about alcohol are the opposite of facts. But just as it is with all people, the personal beliefs of problem drinkers make up a large part of their minds; their minds (through their brains) control their voluntary behavior, including their drinking habits. Therefore, **to help the problem drinkers help themselves most quickly, you must understand both the objective facts about alcohol described in this book and the contrary beliefs problem drinkers have about them.**

The three problem drinkers described in this chapter are typical of the types most likely to solve their drinking problem with The New Self-Help Alcoholic Treatment Method. As you read their case histories, **look for the personal hopes and fears that pulled and pushed them from social drinking, to habitual problem drinking, to alcoholism.**

FIRST CLINICAL CASE SUMMARY

Mrs. Green* was a 57-year-old high school principal. When she came for intensive treatment with The New Self-Help Method, she had been abusing alcohol for six years. During each of the prior four years she had been hospitalized at least once (in out-of-state hospitals) to be dried out. She never sought help in her hometown. Her drinking problem might have come to the attention of her school board members, who might have been forced to fire her.

---

*The names and other identifying data of all of the clinical examples presented in this book have been changed to protect the patients' privacy.

NIGHT CAPS FOR THE LONELY

Dr. M.: Tell me about your drinking problem. When did it start?

Mrs. G.: Well, I guess you could say drinking became a problem for me about eight years ago. I never will forget that year; everything seemed to happen at once.

Dr. M.: Oh? What specifically?

Mrs. G.: Don't misunderstand me; it wasn't anything bad. Actually, I should have been the happiest person you could think of, and I guess I was to some extent. I had finally gotten promoted to a principal, after fighting for twenty years to get it. Before, every other time I thought I'd get it, they had always given it to a man. Then I finally made it, and that was long before all this fuss about ERA. And Charles, Jr. won a full academic scholarship to college. My oldest son graduated from medical school; we had paid off our mortgage the year before. I mean, we were sitting pretty. My husband said, "Vira, honey, we have got it made. Now we can relax and live a little." You know, do all the things we, rather he, always wanted to do but we never had the money for.

Dr. M.: Oh? Like what?

Mrs. G.: Well, the first thing he did was buy the most expensive set of golf clubs he could find, and that was almost the last I saw of him. I mean, before we used to all get home about the same time every day and eat, talk, watch TV, play monopoly, or something like that. But after Charles, Jr. went off to college, Chuck was either taking golf lessons or playing it; and when he wasn't doing that he was out in his new boat fishing. And I hate golf and I'm scared to death of water; so all of a sudden, practically every day I was all alone with tons of time on my hands in a big, empty house. For the first time in my life, I learned what it was like to be lonely. I just felt like everybody was busy enjoying themselves but me. There wasn't anything for me to do with myself.

Dr. M.: Nothing to do?

Mrs. G.: Well, in retrospect, I guess there was a lot I could have done. But, nothing seemed to interest me. I had always gotten my satisfaction from doing things for my husband and children; but then all of a sudden, they weren't there, and I just didn't know what to do with myself. So, I started to nag, something I'd never done before.

Dr. M.: Nag?

Mrs. G.: You know, "Why don't you spend some time at home; how come you have so much time to chase a stupid ball around, but never any time for me?" Stuff like that.

Dr. M.: How did your husband react to that?

Mrs. G.: He just laughed and said: "Vira, baby, what you need is a hobby or a pet; why not both?" So he went out and bought me this expensive little French poodle, but I was allergic to the darn thing and had to get rid of it.

Dr. M.: And then what?

Alcohol For Sleep

Mrs. G.: Well, the more I nagged, the less Chuck was at home. It got so bad that we lived in the same house for two whole weeks without seeing each other even once. We'd leave little (smile) "love" notes; well, one or two were little sweet nothings. I mean, don't get me wrong; Chuck and I really have a good marriage. Never any stepping out on either's part. He really loves me, I know; and I love him, too. But, I just felt left out, worthless. I didn't want to eat, I couldn't sleep. And that's what really got me—not sleeping. I'm the type who has to have her sleep; otherwise, I just can't function. And I had this new job with all that responsibility. That's what started me drinking. I couldn't sleep and I was afraid of sleeping pills. My roommate in college killed herself with them, and I was always afraid of them.

Dr. M.: You didn't drink before that?

Mrs. G.: Oh, a glass of wine with dinner now and then, but that was all.

WHAT DID MRS. GREEN HOPE FOR?

At first it was only restful sleep; later she hoped for sleep plus freedom from painful loneliness. **And there are two things alcohol usually does quickly and reliably: makes painful loneliness seem less painful and induces sleep.**

Mrs. Green's story is quite common. When people first start to drink, nightcaps are fast, painless ways to get to sleep. In addition, Mrs. Green quickly discovered that nightcaps can make being alone more bearable; in fact, she began to enjoy being alone.

Unfortunately, the longer people try to handle their hopes and fears with alcohol, the more alcohol they require; and the more they require, the more likely they are to create drinking problems. Mrs. Green demonstrated that process well.

SECOND CLINICAL CASE SUMMARY

After twenty years of excessive drinking, Dr. Ryan's wife decided enough was enough; either he would have to solve his drinking problem or she would divorce him.

At that time, Dr. Ryan was a 50-year-old career military surgeon. He had failed to benefit from several traditional alcohol treatment programs. Each time, he had quit without really getting involved.

Dr. Ryan said, "I just couldn't accept the idea that I wasn't in control of myself and my life. So what if I had a bit of a drinking problem? I don't see how giving up would help me."

Dr. Ryan was typical of most male and many female problem drinkers we see at the Training Center for Emotional Self-Help. They are intelligent, competent, and self-supporting in spite of their drinking problem. THEY ASSOCIATE GIVING UP WITH BEING A SKID-ROW BUM. THAT SELF-IMAGE IS JUST UNACCEPTABLE TO THEM.

Dr. R.: I'd say I began to drink a little too much, say, roughly five years ago. Before that, I was a social drinker. My wife had to drive me home once in a while, you know, stuff like that, nothing serious. I guess my biggest fault, if you want to call it a fault, is that I'm a lousy monitor.

Dr. M.: I see. Tell me, in what situations have you been most likely to drink too much?

Dr. R.: Parties where there is a lot of activity. I'm sort of a jazz drummer type. I love jazz and I have lots of musical friends; we go to parties with banjos, ukeleles, thump buckets, and just have a ball. I'm known as a clown after I've had a few. But, it's just having fun, you know; but sometimes, I guess I sort of get a little carried away.

Dr. M.: Is that what you mean about lousy monitoring?
Dr. R.: Yeah, I get to thinking: "Hey! I'm having a ball; who cares if I drink a little?" The music sounds better after a few drinks; I play better; and then I guess I get a little carried away; I don't monitor the drinks too well. I mean, the numbers don't mean a thing any more; after all, who cares? I mean people have to enjoy themselves, too; that's how I see it. Now you tell me, Doc, is that all bad?

At this point, I could see that Dr. Ryan tended to minimize his drinking behavior. That habit makes it easier for problem drinkers to justify their excessive drinking to themselves. But I saw no point in making a therapeutic issue of that at this time.

Alcohol To Wash Away Anger

Dr. M.: I see; but you don't have parties every day, right?
Dr. R.: Right.
Dr. M.: So what daily events have been likely to end up with you getting drunk?
Dr. R.: Duress, or stressful situations.
Dr. M.: What type of stress?
Dr. R.: Well, I have a son who has not given me too much reason to shout with joy. But I'm not laying it all on him. I'm just saying—okay, let's start with work.
Dr. M.: Okay, tell me about your work.
Dr. R.: I have problems with people in authority. I know that sounds silly for a career military man; but it's just difficult for me to take orders. I can't stand to have rigid unreasonable people in power over me, forcing me to do things. It just makes me furious.
Dr. M.: Oh? Would you expand on that a bit?
Dr. R.: Well, if you boil it down, it gets down to a simple matter of power—his power over my power.
Dr. M.: In these power conflicts, what do you see the other person doing, or trying to do to you?
Dr. R.: This may sound silly, too, because it could never or would

never happen—I mean, this is the twentieth century, we are civilized and all that—but it's like he's killing me.

Dr. M.: How do you mean?

Dr. R.: It's like, if I give in, he would be killing me.

Dr. M.: Be killing you?

Dr. R.: Right. In other words, he would be wiping me out. If you want to break it down to how it really seems, it's like he would be annihilating me professionally, personally, or whatever.

Dr. M.: How do you react to that perception?

Dr. R.: I want to fight back; but I can't do that. You know, in my situation you can't do that; not in the military. So, I am powerless. (Pause) So, you see, for a variety of reasons, I have to keep myself under tight control; and drinking, well, it helps ease the pressure.

THE HUMAN BRAIN WORKS LIKE A CAMERA

That's why you don't really see this page in front of you. What you see is a mental image of it, created in the back of your brain. BUT, UNLIKE A REAL CAMERA, THE HUMAN BRAIN CAN CREATE A MENTAL IMAGE OF WHAT'S NOT ACTUALLY THERE.

To prove that psychophysiologic fact to yourself, close your eyes now for thirty seconds and picture yourself looking in your bathroom mirror. Do that right now.

You were able to create that image of yourself because of the next psychosomatic fact.

WORDS ARE THE MAIN VEHICLES
OF HUMAN THOUGHT

Your verbs and nouns, especially those that refer to familiar people, objects, or actions, trigger mental images. And the more emotionally aroused you are, the more likely your nouns and action verbs are to trigger life-like mental images.

FORCE VERSUS CHOICE

Like most Rebels-Without-A-Cause, when Dr. Ryan received an order that he didn't like, he would think: "I have to." In fact, though, he didn't have to; he was just afraid not to. And he would get angry at himself for being afraid. But he would carry out the order, because in his mind he was being forced to carry it out.

Always, however, the objective fact had been, he had chosen to carry out the order. Unfortunately, inside the HUMAN BRAIN there are no objective facts—ONLY THOUGHTS AND MENTAL IMAGES, and people can change them to whatever they prefer.

Dr. Ryan's thoughts and images of being forced to do hated tasks triggered intensely painful anger. For that painful emotion to make logical sense to him, he had to maintain his hostile mental images, even though he knew they were inappropriate. Otherwise, his painful anger would have seemed inappropriate. But Dr. Ryan would not consider that possibility; his painful anger felt too logical and right to be inappropriate. So he confused himself even more by thinking "I'm not crazy; I wouldn't be this damn mad if they really weren't trying to do me in." Those beliefs made Dr. Ryan's anger appear to be objective proof that his superior officers really were trying to wipe him out.

THE REBEL-WITHOUT-A-CAUSE SYNDROME

In psychological terms, Dr. Ryan had been projecting his hostile thoughts and feelings onto his superior officers; that mental maneuver enabled him to perceive them as dangerous threats to his life. **But because Dr. Ryan was not psychotic, he knew it would be crazy to act on those perceptions.** Unfortunately though, INSIGHT ALONE DOES NOT ELIMINATE INTENSELY PAINFUL ANGRY FEELINGS; BUT ALCOHOL CAN. So, Dr. Ryan let alcohol do it, again and again, until he created a drinking problem.

HISTORY OF AN ADOLESCENT PROBLEM DRINKER

When Bob came for treatment with the new self-help method, he had been drinking habitually since age fourteen and alcoholically since age eighteen. Then, at age twenty-nine, he had decided that life as a problem drinker was not worth the personal price he had to pay. His wife had left him, taking their two young boys; he was out of work and in legal trouble.

ALCOHOL TO FIT IN WITH THE CROWD

Dr. M.: What did you like about drinking?
Bob: The effects.
Dr. M.: The effects? What about the effects?
Bob: It gave me the feeling that I can do things that I can't do when I'm sober. For example, I could express myself better. I had always had the tendency to be kind of shy, but when I was drinking I could communicate better. I felt like I could fit in the crowd better and be like the rest of the guys.
Dr. M.: And you could maybe make better time with the girls?
Bob: Well, yeah. (Laughs) That was probably the biggest part of it at first.

WHAT IT MEANS TO BE SHY

Bob said he had a tendency to be shy. When an American male says "shy", he usually means painfully afraid of being rejected by females.

The phrase "and be like the other guys" indicated Bob had similar fears about possible rejection by his male friends.

People, especially males, usually feel less miserable about believing they **can't** do something than they feel about being **irrationally afraid** to do it. That's why male problem drinkers usually say: "I can't" when "I'm afraid" would be more accurate.

Irrational fears of rejection usually reveal a negative self-image and intense self-dislike. Therefore, it seemed most logical to say that **Bob started drinking because of curiosity; but, he kept on drinking because of his HOPE to avoid his irrational fear of rejection and painful self-dislike.**

TWO IMPORTANT QUESTIONS

(1) DO ALL PROBLEM DRINKERS DRINK TO GET BETTER EMOTIONAL FEELINGS?
No. But, those who do are most likely to be able to solve their drinking problem with The New Self-Help Alcoholic Treatment Method.

(2) WHAT PERCENT OF THE TEN MILLION HABITUAL PROBLEM DRINKERS DRINK PRIMARILY TO FEEL BETTER EMOTIONALLY?
Recent research indicates that OVER 70 percent (about seven million habitual problem drinkers) drink primarily to get a better emotional feeling. **The ten most common negative feelings problem drinkers hope their alcoholic drinking will improve are: depression, nervousness, worry, just feeling bad, sadness, boredom, stress, anger, shame, and guilt.**

EMPHASIS QUESTIONS FOR CHAPTER ONE

1. Problem drinkers cannot control whether they take a drink or not. True or False?
2. Problem drinkers repeatedly drink to excess for the same reason most people repeatedly do the things they do. True or False?
3. The personal _____ and _____ of otherwise normal people motivate them to drink.
4. Problem drinkers can be taught how to handle their hopes and fears without alcohol. True or False?
5. At first, Mrs. Green drank nightcaps because she hoped for restful _____.
6. Later, Mrs. Green hoped for sleep plus freedom from _____.
7. Dr. Ryan drank out of hope for relief from intense _____.
8. Dr. Ryan really was trapped in this work situation. True or False?
9. Bob started to drink because of _____.
10. Bob kept on drinking because he hoped to avoid his irrational _____ of rejection and intense _____-_____.

11. Many problem drinkers drink to get better emotional feelings. True or False?
12. People who do habitually drink to get better emotional feelings are most likely to solve their drinking problem with _____ New _____-Help _____ Treatment _____.
13. For many problem drinkers alcohol is _____ their main _____; their main problem is excessive _____ emotions that alcohol _____ or _____ temporarily.
14. Recent research indicated that over 70 percent of problem drinkers drink to get a better emotional feeling. True or False?
15. List four common feelings problem drinkers hope their alcoholic drinking will improve:
    (A) _____
    (B) _____
    (C) _____
    (D) _____

CORRECT ANSWERS

1. False
2. True
3. hopes, fears
4. True
5. sleep
6. loneliness
7. anger
8. False
9. curiosity
10. fears, self-dislike
11. True
12. The, Self-, Alcoholic, Method
13. not, problem, negative, dulls, eliminates
14. True
15. depression, nervousness, worry, feeling bad, loneliness, boredom, stress, shame, guilt

2

The Process of Alcohol Addiction

Don't problem drinkers know that too much drinking too often is bad for them? Of course they know it; almost every American (age eight to eighty) knows that too much alcohol too often **causes alcoholism and numerous other personal problems.**

Early problem drinkers almost never believe they are drinking too much, too often. Instead they believe that they are drinking just enough at just the right time. And in one sense they are right. That's because they usually drink to feel better emotionally than they feel in their sober state. For them therefore, just enough alcohol at just the right time **means enough alcohol to get a little drunk.** That fact separates problem drinkers from social drinkers.

At most cocktail parties there are usually at least two people who want to tell a friend: "Hey, you've been drinking too much lately. If you don't cut down, the first thing you know you'll be an alcoholic." Usually though, these people don't say anything. They know that such talk doesn't stop people from drinking too much. But it sure does cause them to change friends fast.

DRINKING STOP AND GO SIGNS FOR ALCOHOL DRINKERS

Sociable and social drinkers usually prefer their sober emotions to alcohol-induced emotions. Either they are satisfied with their sober emotions, or they choose to improve them by other means than excessive drinking. That fact makes **feeling the effects of alcohol** the drinking STOP SIGN for sociable and social drinkers. They don't like feeling drunk; so they stop drinking before they get that way.

But problem drinkers want relief from their sober emotions. And they believe that being a little drunk will give it to them, quick and easy. So they drink until they get that way. That fact makes **feeling the effects of alcohol the drinking** GO SIGN for problem drinkers.

BEHAVIORAL RESEARCH SHOWS

Repeated acts that produce quick relief rapidly become strong behavioral habits. That powerful and reliable learning process is called **negative reinforcement.** When people habitually drink to feel better, negative reinforcement quickly puts them in:

STAGE ONE OF HABITUAL PROBLEM DRINKING

This is the stage of **mental dependence** and **obsession with drinking** to feel better. Then almost any negative emotion is a strong mental cue for alcoholic thinking and problem drinking.

Because problem drinkers have not learned the habit of feeling better without alcohol, they make problem drinking their habit. That habit leads to problems in their family, work and community, and ultimately to the disease called ALCOHOLISM.

ALCOHOLIC BLACK-OUTS (i.e. temporary losses of memory while drinking) are the **first signs of beginning changes from stage one to stage two of problem drinking.** That's also the point where the New Self-Help Treatment Method can most easily stop and reverse the process of alcohol addiction, thereby enabling the drinkers to:
1. Prevent the medical disease—ALCOHOLISM; and
2. Easily return to social drinking.

STAGE TWO OF HABITUAL PROBLEM DRINKING

This is the stage of **physical dependence** and **compulsive drinking. It's the accidental,** but **unavoidable,** end for chronically miserable people who drink alcohol to feel better. The following discussion will give you clear insight into why that accident is unavoidable.

INTERNAL BALANCE AND PHYSICAL WELL BEING

The healthy human body feeds and regulates its vital organ systems (gastrointestinal, cardio-vascular, respiratory, etc.) with the balanced chemical systems of the blood and other bodily fluids. The healthy body's self-regulatory mechanisms keep both the chemical and organ systems in relatively constant, comfortable balance. That state of internal bodily balance is called physiologic homeostasis.

People experience healthy physiologic homeostasis as the relatively calm or pleasantly neutral state of physical and emotional well being. Sudden or **severe changes in physiologic homeostasis** usually cause **severe physical and emotional discomforts.** Such discomforts usually stimulate people to act immediately to restore their bodies to their usual homeostatic state.

ALCOHOL IS AN ADDICTIVE DRUG*

Like most addictive drugs, **alcohol interacts with the chemical systems of the body.** If those interactions are mild and short-term, the body neutralizes and eliminates the alcohol without the drinkers even noticing it. That's why social drinkers usually don't feel any effects from a glass of wine with dinner.

---

*Alcohol is only one of many addictive drugs. But what is true of alcohol is basically true of the many other addictive drugs, including minor tranquilizers, tobacco and narcotics. But people choose their particular addiction according to their personal values and personality traits; that's why the typical problem drinker is usually a different personality type from the typical narcotic addict.

But prolonged, intense interactions between the body and alcohol cause severe imbalances in the body's chemical systems. Those imbalances cause imbalances in the interactions of the vital organ systems and disturb physiologic homeostasis. Alcohol drinkers experience that disturbance as the signs and symptoms of alcohol intoxication. Even so, if the body's self-regulatory systems keep neutralizing and eliminating the alcohol, they ultimately re-establish the usual homeostatic state.

That self-protective mechanism would solve drinkers' problem completely IF alcohol were not an addictive drug.

Unfortunately though, alcohol is an addictive drug. That's why when people frequently expose their bodies to excessive amounts of alcohol for long periods of time this important event occurs: Their bodies begin to treat alcohol as if it were one of the required chemicals for homeostasis.

That event causes serious problems, because the bodies of such drinkers continue to neutralize and eliminate alcohol. Therefore, to maintain comfortable homeostasis, these drinkers must then keep a certain amount of alcohol in their bodies. That situation is the **first sign of physical dependence** on alcohol. It's also the **first sign of the medical disease called ALCOHOLISM.**

WHY THE EASY WAY GETS HARD

Sobering up can be dangerous for severe alcoholics. The first signs of danger are the disturbing symptoms of alcohol withdrawal called PRIMARY ALCOHOLIC CRAVING.

Primary alcoholic craving is an increasingly painful urge to drink alcohol. The longer alcoholics put off drinking, the stronger and more painful their urge to drink becomes. That increasing pain triggers both obsessive thoughts of drinking and a fearfully intense compulsion to drink alcohol, **even though the alcoholics may not want to drink at all.**

Untreated, primary alcoholic craving continues until alcoholics either:
1. dry out, (i.e., sober up completely) and are cured; or
2. stop their craving by drinking alcohol.

In the early phase of alcoholism, problem drinkers usually take the easy, painless way out—a few quick drinks to stop craving. Unfortunately though, the easy way becomes the most difficult in the end; it makes the alcoholic disease worse.

THOSE IMAGINARY ANIMALS CAN FRIGHTEN ALCOHOLICS TO DEATH

Most people think skidrow bums are the only drinkers who get Delirium Tremens (DT's), but they are wrong.

Millionaires, professors, doctors—anyone who is alcoholic enough—can go into DT's.

The major signs of DT's are intense anxiety, confusion, coarse tremors, disorientation and visual hallucinations of animals—snakes, tigers, bugs, elephants, etc. And if they are not treated, those imaginary animals can kill alcoholics.

FOUR INSIGHTS WORTH REPEATING

First, PROBLEM DRINKERS **are usually normal human beings** who have the irrational habit of abusing alcohol to feel better emotionally.

Second, ALCOHOLICS **are problem drinkers who are physically dependent on alcohol** for comfortable homeostasis.

Third, PHYSICAL DEPENDENCE on alcohol (that is alcoholism) can be cured quickly. Just stop alcoholics from drinking; then prevent their death long enough for them to return to their pre-alcoholic, homeostatic state. Their alcoholism will then be cured.

Fourth, CURING ALCOHOLISM **does not cure the mental dependence on alcohol** that makes habitual problem drinking a way of life.

ALCOHOL TO FUNCTION

Remember, at first, habitual problem drinkers are merely trying to get better emotional feelings. But once their bodies are addicted to alcohol, they drink out of fear of alcoholic withdrawal. That fear causes them to structure their lives around alcohol. Here's how Bob described that transition.

Bob: Anyway, I kept on drinking because I didn't see any harmful effects from it. And not much happened until I was seventeen, when I got married. I guess I bit off a little more than I could chew. I mean when I was single I just had to support my drink and myself. But when I got married, I had to support my drink, myself, my wife, my kids, and in

	that order. I got to the point where I had to drink to go to work, or I'd start shaking. I kept changing jobs, but I was never fired; I was always asked to resign.
Dr. M.:	Oh, why would they ask you to resign?
Bob:	Well, my drinking on the job made me a hazard to the other employees.
Dr. M.:	Oh, I see.

Alcohol To Pay Bills

Bob's frequent changes in jobs kept him chronically short of money. Like most people, he knew that stealing can be a quick, easy way to get money. But, also like most people, Bob's anxiety about going to jail kept him from stealing when he was sober. After he had had a few drinks, however, thoughts of stealing no longer triggered anxiety about going to jail. Without his inhibiting anxiety, stealing seemed like a safe, easy way to get money; so Bob stole welfare checks; and for a while he got away with it.

During that time, alcohol was solving Bob's social problems and his money problems too. That fact doubly reinforced his mental dependence on alcohol as the key to enjoying life.

Alcohol To Make Life Worth Living

Bob:	Drinking just became a part of my daily life; everything I did involved drinking. Even when I went to church, which wasn't too often, but when I did go, I'd still be feeling the effects from the night before, or I'd still have some in my system. And so I kept on drinking, stealing, and pretty soon I got arrested for the first time and sent to jail; and I couldn't get anything to drink then.
Dr. M.:	So, what happened?
Bob:	I got terribly sick from the withdrawal. And after that I got depressed.
Dr. M.:	Depressed?
Bob:	Yeah, I just wanted to give it up, life and everything, because they had taken away the only thing that was really

	important to me.
Dr. M.:	You mean drinking?
Bob:	Right, my drinking.

By now it's probably clear why Bob got depressed about being cured (i.e., dried out) and why problem drinkers stubbornly resist the idea of giving up alcohol completely. To them, completely giving up alcohol means giving up all their joy in life, if not the essence of life itself. As Bob put it: "I figured since I've got to die with something, I may as well die feeling good."

Alcohol To Make The Brain Work Better

Dr. M.: Okay, then what?
Bob: Well, after about two months, I got out on bond. They had told me I was going to get a long sentence, so I figured I'd go back to drinking so I could figure out a way to get out of it.

Even after two months in jail, Bob was still obsessed with the idea that alcohol was his best and most reliable friend when he needed help. He honestly believed his alcoholically-primed brain was better than his sober brain for finding a solution to his legal problem.

Dr. M.: What happened then?
Bob: Well, as it turned out, I didn't have to go to prison; I got a suspended sentence with probation. So, I figured since I got off free, I might as well keep on drinking and enjoy myself. So I did that for a year or so, until I got arrested again. That time I got a three-year sentence. I ended up serving nine months of it before they let me out on parole. (Laugh) And in nine months without a drink I really did dry out.
Dr. M.: Okay, and then what?
Bob: (Laughing) Well, my first day out, I was drunk before I got home.
Dr. M.: (Laughing) How do you explain that?
Bob: I don't know. It's a puzzle to me.

Sober problem drinkers are unhappy people. Alcohol is their way of feeling better emotionally, but that means getting a little bit drunk. Unfortunately, habitually getting a little bit drunk is like getting a little bit pregnant—very soon it becomes a whole lot. That's why most sober alcoholics fail to become social drinkers without expert professional help. Converting the GO SIGN for problem drinking to the drinking STOP SIGN of social drinking requires more self-restraint than most alcoholics seem able to learn without professional guidance.

POSTPONING PROBLEM DRINKING DOESN'T STOP IT

It was obvious to me why Bob got drunk on his first day out of prison—**the legal system had imprisoned his body, but not his mind. Learning to stop drinking** DOES NOT happen in prison; it DOES NOT happen in hospital wards nor in the offices of psychotherapists or physicians. Learning to solve a drinking problem **happens only in the problem drinker's brain.**

Learning to stop drinking may happen while problem drinkers

are locked up in prisons or on hospital wards. But in either case, problem drinkers must do the next two things **before that learning can take place:**

First, they must consistently think thoughts that enable them to stop rather than postpone drinking.

Second, they must habitually act out those thoughts until acting them out becomes habitual.

Before Bob received The New Self-Help Treatment he had never done those two things. When he was out of jail, he was too busy drinking to learn how to stop. And when he was in jail, he passed his idle time by planning his big drinking celebration of getting out.

That's why the day he got out of jail he was just as obsessed as ever with the idea that alcohol was the only way for him to enjoy life and cope with the world.

WHY ABSTINENCE ALONE IS NOT ENOUGH

Jail forced abstinence on Bob, but on their own Mrs. Green and Dr. Ryan sometimes voluntarily abstained from drinking for several weeks at a time. That fact made it easier for them to deny and minimize their problem drinking much longer than Bob could. But, just like Bob, before they received The New Self-Help Alcoholic Treatment, they had never freed themselves from their obsessive idea that when all else failed, alcohol would see them through. Dr. Ryan described his obsession this way:

Dr. M.: Tell me, during those times when you'd keep yourself from drinking by taking Antabuse and refusing to have alcohol in your house, how would you talk yourself into going off Antabuse and then buying more booze?

Dr. R.: Usually it was the other way around.

Dr. M.: Oh? You'd buy the booze, then you'd stop Antabuse?

Dr. R.: Right. You see, I'm a bit of a handyman around the house. My wife says that's why I'm such a good surgeon: I'm so good with my hands; and when I'm sober I'm good, damn good, even if I do say so myself. Anyway, I'm constantly going to the store, the hardware store to get screws, washers, paint, you name it, for the house. And you know, in every shopping center in the world there is a liquor store right next door to the hardware store.

Dr. M.: Oh? I hadn't noticed.

Dr. R.: Yeah, well that's the way it seems in my town. Anyway, so I'm going for the paint and I start telling myself: "You dumb ass; walk by the liquor store and go get your paint and go home." And I usually do; I mean I go straight to the hardware store and buy my paint. But, then I've still got to walk back by the liquor store. So, I'm thinking that maybe I should have at least one bottle around as kind of self-protection.

Dr. M.: Self-protection? Self-protection against what?

Dr. R.: Well (pause) you never know. I mean, in my life, anything just might happen. You never can tell what duress you might find yourself under. So I'm thinking:

Dr. M.: Duress? Duress about what?

Dr. R.: Anything. My son was always a good excuse. I might think: "What if Jack is planning to come put the bite on his poor mother again. It's about time. We haven't heard from him in three or four months. That's about how long it usually takes him to forget the last jam we got him out of." I go on like that for a few seconds.

Dr. M.: Then what?

Dr. R.: Well, the first thing you know, I'm in the liquor store; and I really hate going in liquor stores. I think it's the dumbest goddamn thing in the world.

Dr. M.: When you are actually there, or just in retrospect?

Dr. R.: (Pause, then smiling) I guess I have to say it's in retrospect because at the time, I just rush in, buy it, rush out, and start trying to think of where I can hide it from Peggy, my wife.

Dr. M.: Then what?

Dr. R.: Well, after I hide it, I begin to think: "I don't need this damn Antabuse. It's all psychological; it doesn't have any pharmacological effect on me. If I can tell myself 'I can't drink' after taking it, I can tell myself the same thing without taking it. There's no magic in that pill. It's still me doing it." So I stop taking the pill, mainly to prove that I'm my own man and that I still control me.

Dr. M.: And then you'd wait until Jack visited you again?

Dr. R.: Well, yeah (smiling) if he didn't take too long. But you know how it is in the military; there is always something to bug you.

THE PROBLEM DRINKER'S BLIND SPOT

The main insight to make here is that Dr. Ryan never once decided that alcohol was bad for him. Sure he hated the liquor store, but you don't have to like sleeping in a pigpen to enjoy pork chops. **The point is: Dr. Ryan was convinced that when things, or life in general, really got tough, he needed—in fact, he had to have—his booze to help him survive.** That is the essence of being in the stage of mental dependence on alcohol.

WHAT PROBLEM DRINKERS NEED

To stop abusing alcohol permanently, they need to stop being mentally dependent on alcohol to cope with life; **the New Self-Help Treatment Method is one quick, easy way** for them to stop. That's because it teaches problem drinkers to do Rational Self-Counseling.

RATIONAL SELF-COUNSELING (RSC)

That's the name of the New Self-Help Alcoholic Treatment Method. The remainder of this book describes it and gives you step-by-step, detailed instructions in how to use it as well as teach it.

WHO'S APPROPRIATE FOR RSC?

Only problem drinkers who have the following four characteristics:

1. They admit that they created and are maintaining their drinking problem, and that only they can get rid of it.

2. They drink primarily because they hope to get a better emotional feeling and/or they are afraid of getting a worse one.

3. They accept these two facts: a) drying out solves ONLY half of their drinking problem; b) solving the other half means learning to control their hopes, fears and other emotions to their satisfaction without problem drinking.

4. They are willing to dry out and stay sober while they learn how to control their emotions to their satisfaction with Rational Self-Counseling alone.

EMPHASIS QUESTIONS FOR CHAPTER TWO

1. Habitual drinkers usually believe they are drinking too much. True or False?
2. Social drinkers prefer their sober emotions to their alcohol-induced emotions. True or False?
3. The drinking _____ light for social drinkers is the drinking _____ light for problem drinkers.
4. Problem drinkers continue to drink excessively because of the fast, easy way alcohol temporarily _____ their unwanted emotions.
5. Alcohol is the best way to improve emotional well-being. True or False?
6. The two stages of problem drinking are the stage of mental dependence and obsession with drinking and the stage of _____ dependence and compulsive drinking.
7. The normal state of balance in the chemical and organ systems of the body is called _____ _____.
8. When people abuse alcohol frequently enough their bodies begin to need alcohol to maintain feelings of physical well-being. True or False?

9. When a person is in the second stage of problem drinking or physiologic dependence, just sobering up causes disturbing symptoms of alcohol withdrawal called primary _____ craving.
10. Compulsive drinking is drinking because of an urge to drink even when you sincerely don't want to drink. True or False?
11. Fear of _____ _____ is one reason alcoholics compulsively structure their lives around alcohol.
12. Medically speaking, once problem drinkers are _____ up and out of danger of _____, their physiologic dependence or the compulsive stage of their drinking problem is over.
13. After having been withdrawn from alcohol in jail, Bob was happy. True or False?
14. Bob got drunk on his first day out of prison because they had imprisoned his _____, but not his _____.
15. Learning to stop drinking happens only in the problem drinker's _____.
16. In order to solve a drinking problem, people must _____ to solve the problem and consistently _____ thoughts that when acted out, prevent problem drinking.
17. To solve a drinking problem, problem drinkers must learn to control their hopes, _____, and other _____ without alcohol.

CORRECT ANSWERS

1. False
2. True
3. stop, go
4. lessens, dulls, decreases, stops, etc.
5. False
6. physiologic or physical
7. physiologic homeostasis
8. True
9. alcoholic
10. True
11. withdrawal symptoms
12. sobered, DT's
13. False
14. body, brain
15. brain
16. desire, think
17. fears, emotions

Rational Self-Counseling for Problem Drinkers

A COMMON QUESTION

Can you trust problem drinkers to counsel themselves? YES! You not only can trust them to do it; you can't stop them, even if you wanted to. Self-Counseling is the ONLY kind people can follow. It doesn't matter where people get their ideas: from mental health professionals, books, radio, TV, church or wherever. Before ideas can influence their behavior, they must accept those ideas; then they must direct themselves to follow them. Once people accept and follow ideas, those ideas are theirs. That's why SELF-COUNSELING IS THE ONLY EFFECTIVE KIND.

The important questions physicians, psychotherapists and alcohol counselors need to answer are:

WHAT IS RATIONAL SELF-COUNSELING?

It's a comprehensive, self-help method that enables people to solve their personal problems faster with the rational use of their healthy brains than they can with alcohol or other legal or illegal drugs. Rational Self-Counseling has that power because science has not yet enabled man to improve on nature at its best; and the healthy, undrugged human brain is an example of nature at its best.

Rational Self-Counseling or RSC is comprehensive because it deals directly with the three main groups of habitual human behaviors: **habits of perceiving and thinking**, or COGNITIVE behaviors; **habits of emotional feelings**, or EMOTIVE behaviors; and **habits of voluntary action**, or PHYSICAL behaviors.

WHEN IS SELF-COUNSELING RATIONAL?

Self-counseling is rational when it clearly obeys three or more of the following five rules for optimal mental and emotional health.

1. It is based on obvious facts.
2. It helps you protect yourself from probable harm.
3. It helps you achieve your short-term and long-term goals.
4. It helps you avoid significant conflict with other people.

(Significant conflict is the amount you decide for yourself to act to avoid.)

5. It helps you habitually feel the emotions you want to feel.

Why are these the rules for mental and emotional health? BECAUSE:

1. People whose cognitive, emotive, and physical behaviors consistently obey three or more of these five rules almost always maintain or improve their mental and emotional health.
2. People whose cognitive, emotive, and physical behaviors consistently disobey three or more of these five rules almost always have a major psychiatric disorder.

With those two facts in mind, take a few moments now to review the five rules more thoughtfully. That's the best way to convince yourself of their value.

THE FIVE RULES FOR RATIONAL SELF-COUNSELING

1. It is based on obvious facts.
2. It helps you protect yourself from probable harm.
3. It helps you achieve your short and long-term goals.
4. It helps you avoid significant conflict with other people. (Significant conflict is the amount you decide for yourself to act to avoid.)
5. It helps you habitually feel the emotions you want to feel.

WHEN IS SELF-COUNSELING IRRATIONAL?

That's easy to tell. Irrational Self-Counseling clearly disobeys three or more of the five rules for Rational Self-Counseling.

THE MAIN SCIENTIFIC ASSUMPTIONS IN RATIONAL SELF-COUNSELING

1. The world is a nonmagical place in which events occur only when what is necessary for them to occur has been done.
2. When what is necessary for an event to occur has been done, that event has to and therefore should occur.

PSYCHOSOMATIC FACTS SUPPORTING RATIONAL SELF-COUNSELING

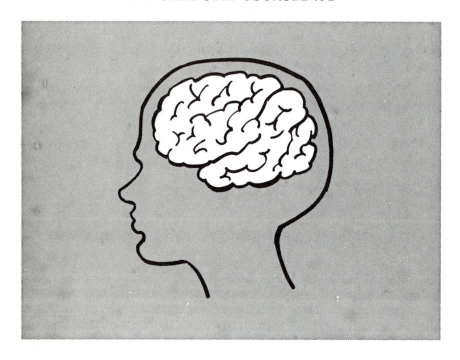

1. The brain is the main site of learning and control of voluntary behavior.
2. The human mind, through the brain and spinal cord (Central Nervous System), controls learned behaviors by directing and coordinating the activities of the autonomic and peripheral nervous system.
3. The human mind consists largely of semi-permanent mental units, or cognitive habits, called beliefs and attitudes. These cognitive

habits individually and jointly (through the brain) direct the autonomic and peripheral nervous system in controlling emotional and physical reactions.

4. The words (mainly nouns, verbs, and adjectives) people use to describe their personal beliefs are autoconditioned (self-taught) mental cues used by their brains for triggering and controlling their specific emotional and physical reactions.

5. Human motivation for voluntarily repeated acts is largely HOPE for something wanted, FEAR of something unwanted, or some combination of these two emotions.

RATIONAL SELF-ANALYSIS AND RATIONAL EMOTIVE IMAGERY

They are the main self-help techniques used in Rational Self-Counseling. Usually, people can learn them as quickly as they can learn any new habits. **And once people start using these self-help techniques daily, they start helping themselves to as much happiness as possible** in the shortest time possible for them.

Rational Self-Analysis or RSA does two important things:

1. It clearly shows people the part they habitually play in causing both their desirable and undesirable life experiences.

AND

2. It tells people the most rational changes to make in their behavior to get rid of, or avoid irrational life experiences.

Rational Emotive Imagery or REI enables people to replace their undesirable emotional and physical habits with more desirable ones in the shortest possible time.

WHY RATIONAL SELF-COUNSELING IS IDEAL FOR PROBLEM DRINKERS

Six years and over a half-million dollars in research and testing at the Training Center for Rational Behavior Therapy and Emotional Self-Help (University of Kentucky Medical College, Lexington, Kentucky) indicate that Rational Self-Counseling (RSC) has the six ideal features of a self-help method for problem drinkers. These features are:

1. It is based on recent research data about problem drinkers and their problems.
2. It is easy to learn quickly.
3. It is practical, effective, and economical.
4. It eliminates the causes of problem drinking and prevents people from returning to it.
5. It is easy for physicians, psychotherapists and trained lay people to teach to problem drinkers.
6. It makes treating sober problem drinkers on an out-patient or day-hospital basis MORE efficient, effective, and economical than treating them on an in-patient basis.

EMPHASIS QUESTIONS

1. The best type of self-counseling for problem drinkers is _____ to learn.
2. The best type of self-counseling for problem drinkers is practical, effective, and economical. True or False?
3. Rational Self-Counseling is a comprehensive self-_____ method that enables people to solve their personal problems faster without _____ than they can with them.
4. Rational Self-Counseling enables problem drinkers to eliminate the _____ of their _____ drinking.
5. Rational Self-Counseling deals with the three main groups of human behavior. True or False?
6. Those three groups of human behaviors are: _____, emotive, and _____ behaviors.
7. Behavior is rational if it obeys _____ of the five rules for optimal mental health.
8. Rational behavior is based on _____ and helps you _____ yourself from probable _____.
9. Rational thinking helps you achieve only your short-term goals. True or False?
10. "Significant" conflict with other people means the amount of conflict you decide to act to _____

11. In RSC, "irrational behavior" refers to cognitive, emotive, and physical behaviors that disobey three or more of the five rules for Rational Self-Counseling. True or False?
12. The _____ is the main site of learning and control of human behaviors.
13. Attitudes and beliefs are cognitive _____.
14. Human motivation for voluntarily repeated behavior consists largely of _____ for something wanted, _____ of something unwanted or a _____ of those two emotions.
15. The only kind of counseling that people can follow is _____ counseling.

CORRECT ANSWERS

1. easy
2. True
3. help, drugs or alcohol
4. causes, problem
5. True
6. cognitive, physical
7. three
8. facts, protect, harm
9. False
10. avoid
11. True
12. brain
13. habits
14. hope, fear, combination
15. self

SECTION II

(Part One)

The following chapters give you more basic facts and insights about problem drinking, plus step-by-step instructions for learning, using and teaching them to others.

    Chapter 4 The ABC's of Alcoholic Self-Help

    Chapter 5 Are Your Emotions Really As Simple As That?

    Chapter 6 Why Thoughts are More Important Than Emotional Feelings

    Chapter 7 The Rational Use of Your Emotional ABC's

    Chapter 8 Wanting Versus Craving a Drink

    Chapter 9 Teaching Cured Alcoholics About Alcohol Addiction

Remember, the quickest way to get the most from your reading is to GET INVOLVED IN EACH CHAPTER BEFORE YOU READ IT. The second paragraph on page 8 describes a simple way to get deeply involved in a chapter quickly and easily.

4

The ABC's of Alcoholic Self-Help

Thinking is the single most important act humans normally do. It directs all of their voluntary behavior. Yet, people usually pay much more attention to their emotional feelings than to their thoughts. That's the main reason problem drinking quickly becomes habitual. Problem drinkers like the way alcohol dulls their emotional pain. That's also the main reason they refuse to stop abusing alcohol until they learn to feel better emotionally without it.

Learning the emotional ABC's is the first step in learning to feel better without alcohol or other drugs. That's why it's the first self-help step in the New Self-Help Alcoholic Treatment Method.

THE EMOTIONAL ABC'S

Emotional feelings are probably the most talked about yet misunderstood of all human reactions. Every day millions of **people accuse he, she or they of upsetting them**, or of making them feel good. And if they have no other people to accuse, they accuse IT—the external world. Sometimes they claim that it upsets them, and other times they claim that it makes them feel good. In both cases, however, they are mistaken; they really don't know why their emotional feelings happen, nor who nor what makes them happen. That's why so many of these people try to feel better by abusing alcohol, tranquilizers, and other legal and illegal drugs. But after such people learn PSYCHOSOMATIC FACT #1, they realize that they can have pleasant emotions without abusing drugs. **They then see that neither other people nor external things cause human emotional feelings.**

Psychosomatic Fact #1
PEOPLE CAUSE THEIR OWN EMOTIONAL FEELINGS BY THE WAY THEY USE THEIR MINDS

At first, many people resist accepting Psychosomatic Fact #1. It doesn't feel right to them to think they cause their own emotional pain. Their objection is both normal and understandable. New facts usually seem wrong when they disagree with old beliefs.

For example, most people laughed when the first person said:

But now the only people who laugh are naive children and babbling idiots. That fact brings me to a very important insight:

Emotional Insight #1
MUCH OF WHAT EVERYBODY KNOWS IS JUST NOT WORTH KNOWING!

Fortunately, recent medical research makes one fact very clear: if you are physically normal, **you create, you maintain, and you eliminate your own emotional feelings**—whether positive, negative, or neutral.

Why is that fact fortunate? Because if you accept it, you free yourself to learn these two important skills: how to stop having emotions you don't like to have, and how to create emotions you do like to have.

Are these skills hard to learn? No! Just accept the psychosomatic facts and emotional insights described here, and then use them in your daily life. **Daily use will make these skills come easily and quickly!**

The psychosomatic facts described in this book apply to all normal people. Since you're normal, apply Psychosomatic Fact #1 to yourself right now. Before you have a new emotion, what do you usually do first? You notice something; you perceive some real event, or you imagine or remember one. Second, you have sincere evaluative thoughts about what your perceptions mean to you or about you.

There are only three major types of evaluative thoughts: relatively positive, relatively negative, and relatively neutral. These evaluative thoughts trigger and control your relatively positive, relatively negative and relatively neutral emotional feelings. These are psychophysiologic facts; that's why they are the basis of the ABC's of alcoholic (and all other rational) self-help.

Now let's apply these facts and insights to real-life events.

First, **Harry**, a habitual problem drinker, saw a bottle.

He sincerely thought: "Boy that sure looks good. I can taste it already."

Harry's sincere positive thoughts about drinking triggered POSITIVE emotional feelings and POSITIVE physical actions for drinking. So he bought the bottle, carried it home and drank it.

Now we can talk objectively about:

THE ABC'S OF YOUR NEW POSITIVE EMOTIONS

A. Your Perceptions or What You Notice;
   PLUS
B. Your Sincere POSITIVE Thoughts About Your Perceptions;
   PLUS
C. Your POSITIVE Gut or Emotional Feelings, Triggered and Maintained by Your Positive Evaluative Thoughts.

Psychosomatic Fact #2
THE BRAIN IS THE MAIN HUMAN ORGAN OF PERCEPTIONS AND THOUGHTS

That fact put your brain in direct control of your emotional feelings. You probably knew that fact already, but like most people you probably ignore it. You probably think: "So what? I can't control what my brain does." And you're right: you can't control what your brain does. But—**if you are healthy and undrugged—you do control your mind.** That fact leads to another important insight:

Emotional Insight #2
YOUR SYSTEMS OF HABITUAL PERCEPTIONS AND THOUGHTS ARE ESSENTIAL PARTS OF YOUR MIND

You use those essential parts of your mind to describe which of your perceptions and evaluative thoughts you react to. **So even though you don't control what your brain does, you do control when and how your brain does it.** That's all the control you need to improve your self-control.

Your NEGATIVE EMOTIONS work just like your positive and neutral emotions. They all have the same ABC's.

THE ABC'S OF ALL EMOTIONS

A. Your Perceptions or What You Notice;
   PLUS
B. Your Sincere Evaluative Thoughts About Your Perceptions;
   PLUS
C. Your GUT or Emotional Feelings, Triggered and Maintained by Your Evaluative Thoughts.

Curly, a cured alcoholic, also saw a bottle.

But when he thought about buying it, he remembered the last time he bought a bottle.

Since you know the negative thoughts Curly had about drinking, you are probably not surprised that he said: "It's just not worth it." . . . and calmly walked away.

THE ABC'S OF YOUR NEW NEGATIVE EMOTIONS

A. Your Perceptions, or What You Notice;
   PLUS
B. Your Sincere NEGATIVE Thoughts About Your Perceptions;
   PLUS
C. Your Negative Gut or Emotional Feelings, Triggered and Maintained by Your Negative Evaluative Thoughts.

Your NEUTRAL EMOTIONS are REAL EMOTIONS too. So don't get confused by the popular but incorrect idea of "no emotions." It is medically impossible for a healthy person to be in a state of "no emotions." The state most people mislabel "no emotions" is really the neutral or calm emotional state. When you are in the neutral or calm emotional state, you don't notice any definitely positive or definitely negative emotions. But you are still having real emotional feelings. That's the state doctors call physiologic homeostasis. It's usually the most comfortable and the most productive emotional state. If you don't believe it, try to thread a needle while you are laughing.

Or remember how worn out you feel after worrying about something for three hours. That's why emotionally healthy people keep themselves in the neutral or calm emotional state most of the time. The other states are too emotionally demanding.

Medically speaking, your neutral emotional feelings are similar to your neutral physical feelings. For example, how does your left cheek feel at this moment? Until I asked you about it, you were probably unaware of your left cheek. But did that mean you didn't have any feelings in it? Of course not. You just were not noticing the feelings there.

But suppose you had just left the dentist, and your left cheek was still numb from the anesthesia. Then you really wouldn't have any feelings in your left cheek, and you would be very much aware of it. But what excactly would you be aware of? **You would be aware of not feeling your cheek.** So, you see, **there is a big difference between "no feelings" and not noticing your feeling.**

Helen was a social drinker, sincerely trying to lose weight.

That's why she thought sincere positive, negative, and neutral thoughts about the drinks she saw. Her positive thoughts balanced off her negative thoughts; that fact put her firmly in a neutral emotional state about drinking.

"That liquor would taste good, BUT it would slow down my weight loss. So, the taste would be good, but the overall results would be bad for me."

Helen's sincere neutral thoughts about alcoholic drinks caused her to have neutral emotions toward them. That fact maximally freed her to react neutrally toward them and feel good about doing it.

That scene shows how helpful it is for cured alcoholics to know their emotional ABC's; before learning them, most cured alcoholics believe they have to feel tense about refusing an offered drink. A common description is: "It's really a strain not drinking with your friends. After a while it just gets to be too much." But after cured alcoholics learn their emotional ABC's they see they were mistaken.

Psychosomatic Fact #3
IF YOU KNOW YOUR EMOTIONAL ABC'S, YOU CAN USUALLY FEEL AND ACT THE WAY YOU WANT TO WITHOUT ALCOHOL OR OTHER DRUGS

THE ABC'S OF YOUR NEW NEUTRAL EMOTIONS

A. Your Perceptions, or What You Notice;
 PLUS
B. Your Sincere NEUTRAL or BALANCED Thoughts About Your Perceptions;
 PLUS
C. Your NEUTRAL Gut or Emotional Feelings, Triggered and Maintained by Your Neutral or Balanced Thoughts.

Next is objective proof that: **IT, the outside world, never does anything to human emotions.** Here we have three people looking at the same bottle, but each person has a different emotional feeling about it.

The same facts that free them to feel as they feel, also free you to feel as you feel. **IT, the outside world, never does anything to human emotions; instead, you do everything to your emotions about IT. But—you always have three choices of things to do.** You can create relatively positive emotions, relatively negative emotions, or relatively neutral emotions. That's why if you want to, you can learn how to choose your emotions to your advantage. But REMEMBER:

Psychosomatic Fact #4
EMOTIONAL FEELINGS DON'T WORK LIKE PHYSICAL FEELINGS

IT, the outside world, **can't** cause your emotional feelings. But IT, the outside world, **can** cause your physical feelings. For example, suppose each person had taken a drink of coffee while it was still too hot to drink.

Each person's mouth would have felt the same type of painful burn. That's because IT (in this case, the heat) **really can** cause your physical feelings.

EMPHASIS QUESTIONS

1. This chapter describes how abnormal emotions work. True or False?
2. You really do control your own emotions. True or False?
3. If a new idea feels wrong, it must be wrong. True or False?
4. When you sincerely think an idea, you have a (a) _____ emotional or gut (b) _____ for your idea.
5. In Scene #1, what made Harry feel good? (a) the bottle; (b) his sincere positive thoughts about alcohol; (c) the taste of the alcohol?
6. In Scene #2, what made Curly have negative feelings about the bottle: (a) the bottle; (b) the weather; (c) his sincere negative thoughts and beliefs about past drinking?
7. In Scene #3, what caused Helen to refuse to drink with her friends: (a) she discovered they weren't really her friends; (b) she subconsciously hates alcohol; (c) her sincere neutral or balanced-off thoughts and feelings about drinking while dieting?
8. If everybody knows something, then it must be worth knowing. True or False?
9. Normal people don't have to be emotional slaves to HE, SHE, IT and THEY. True or False?
10. Normally, your heart controls your emotional feelings. True or False?

CORRECT ANSWERS

1. False
2. True
3. False
4. logical, feeling
5. his sincere positive thoughts about alcohol
6. his sincere negative thoughts and beliefs about past drinking
7. her sincere neutral thoughts and feelings about drinking while dieting
8. False
9. True
10. False

5

Are Your Emotions Really as Simple as ABC?

YES!! But at first, many people don't want to believe it. They think to themselves: "I'm fairly intelligent. I studied psychology. If my emotions were really that simple, I would have figured out my ABC's myself." But they didn't figure them out. So they initially want to reject the ABC model; it's not mind-boggling enough. They prefer to believe their emotions are uncontrollable and incomprehensibly complex.

To help such people quickly rid themselves of that nonsense, I help them to see why they missed discovering their emotional ABC's for themselves: **they had the wrong focus.** When they thought about the causes of their emotional feelings, they didn't look at their thoughts; instead, they looked only at the external world.

Why? Probably because their emotional feelings were so intensely distracting. But regardless of the reason, when people focus primarily on the external world to explain their emotional feelings, they remain emotionally naive. Consequently, when they try to analyze their emotions, they're like kids trying to figure out how a TV set works by looking only at the TV picture. But when such people learn Psychosomatic Fact #*5*, they free themselves to get the most correct and the most useful emotional understanding.

Psychosomatic Fact #5
ALMOST ALL HUMAN EMOTIONS ARE AS SIMPLE AS A, B, C

Since repetition is the royal road to rapid learning, let's do a quick review of:

Your Emotional ABC's

A. Your Perceptions or What You Notice;

PLUS

B. Your Sincere Evaluative (positive, negative, or neutral) Thoughts About Your Perceptions;

PLUS

C. Your (positive, negative, or neutral) Gut or Emotional Feelings, Triggered and Maintained by Your Evaluative Thoughts.

Simple emotional ignorance is not the only reason most people initially resist learning their emotional ABC's. Some people go one step further and confuse themselves with misinterpretations of the next three emotional facts:

First, people usually don't have A-B-C type emotions. They rarely first perceive, then think, then get logical emotive feelings.

Second, most people have tried (more than once) to have different emotional feelings about similar external situations and have usually failed.

Third, most often people have A-C or B-C types of emotional reactions. They habitually have either:

A.	Their External Perception and only	OR	B.	Their Evaluative Thoughts and only
C.	Their Emotive Reactions		C.	Their Emotive Reactions

The key concept here is HABIT. People most often react in the way they are in the habit of reacting. **A-C and B-C types of emotions are the most common types because they are habitual emotions.** But, no one starts out with emotional habits. Like all habits, emotional habits have to be LEARNED.

Habit-learning usually requires TIME and diligent PRACTICE. And regardless of the types of habits being learned, people learn them according to the same old A-B-C model:

First, they perceive the task to be learned at A.

Second, they think the evaluative thoughts at B that enable them to perform the task perceived at A.

Third, their B-thoughts trigger logical bodily (emotive and physical) reactions at C.

When people repeat (that is, practice) that sequence enough times, their bodily reactions (at C) gradually become habitual and semi-automatic.

Now, prove to yourself that most habit-learning follows those same A, B, C steps. Study in detail a typical habit most people clearly understand. For example, start with the correct car-driving habit.

First, students perceive a car; that's A.

Second, they think their correct car-driving thoughts; e.g., "The first thing I do is put the gear in park; then I put my foot on the brake and turn on the ignition; next I put the gear in drive, but I keep my foot on the brake until no traffic is coming;" etc. Those are B-evaluative thoughts.

Third, they react at C to those thoughts with logical emotional feelings and the correct physical actions.

At first, his emotional feelings will probably be mild apprehension or anxiety. That's the logical, healthy emotional reaction to a new learning experience, especially one that is potentially dangerous. But with correct practice, he will quickly learn safe, correct driving habits so well that he won't have to consciously think about them anymore to drive correctly. By that time, his continuous correct driving practice will have enabled him to replace his initial anxiety with the calm emotional feelings logical for confidence of success. The next psychosomatic facts explain why and how that happens.

Normally, by repeating the same perceptions, thoughts, emotional feelings, and physical actions, people force their brains to do an important thing. **Their brains convert their repeated perceptions and thoughts into habitual mental units called beliefs and attitudes.**

Your beliefs are the spoken forms of the habitual, A-B type mental connections your brain makes between your repeated perceptions at A and your repeated emotional and physical reactions at C. In spite of the robotlike repetition required to learn beliefs, your beliefs free you from sub-humanlike dependence on the external world for your emotional and physical reactions. After you learn correct driving beliefs, you no longer need a car to practice correct driving; you can sit in your home, do mental practice, and increase your skill in driving.

If you already know how to drive a car, you can quickly prove that fact to yourself right now. Just close your eyes and create a mental picture of yourself driving correctly. Concentrate as intensely as you can while picturing yourself moving your arms and legs through the correct driving motions. If you concentrate enough, you will start to feel calm emotional feelings, logical for the confidence of success you normally have when driving. Stop now and actually do that little experiment.

To do that exercise well, you had to be aware of thinking yourself through the correct driving motions. It was irrelevant that you weren't in a car. You created a car in your mind. Then you thought yourself—that is, you self-talked yourself—through the correct motions of driving it.

Because you have to think your beliefs, you always notice

them. That's an important fact; remember it well: You always notice your beliefs because you have to think them to be sure that you will react (as nearly as is possible) in the way that you want to.

At the same time that the human brain forms beliefs, it also forms attitudes. **Your attitudes are the unspoken form of the habitual, A-B mental connections your brain makes between your repeated perceptions at A and your repeated emotional and physical reactions at C.** In spite of the robot-like repetition required to learn your attitudes, they enable you to have your seemingly spontaneous but correct answers. Your attitudes let you react correctly without first thinking about what you are going to do.

Because attitudes are unspoken beliefs, people usually don't notice them. That's why most people naively explain their attitudinally triggered (or so-called spontaneous) emotional and physical reactions with: "He, she, or it made me feel (or do) it" OR "Something like magic just took over my body and I was powerless to resist."

When such people learn that their emotional habits work just like their driving habits, they stop making such naive excuses for their emotional and physical behavior.

After you learn correct driving attitudes, you don't have to talk yourself through the driving motions to drive correctly. You can then talk to your friends or listen to the radio and still drive correctly. Your unspoken, correct driving attitudes will appropriately coordinate your external perceptions of the driving situation at A with your appropriate emotional and physical reactions at C.

To see what your attitudes are, you must first convert them into their spoken or beliefs form. You can quickly do that by honestly answering this question: "What beliefs did I react as if I thought?"

For example, suppose our student driver were driving his car and suddenly a child runs across the road in front of him. He would probably immediately slam on the brakes and feel afraid, all without taking time to think anything.

By reacting that way, he would have reacted as if he had thought: "I'm about to have a terrible accident; I'd better stop immediately."

But suppose he were driving and sees the same child running down the sidewalk, parallel to the street. Now he would probably continue to maintain his speed and feel calm about doing so, again without consciously thinking anything. Why? Because his controlling attitude would then be the unspoken form of his beliefs: "There is no danger; I have no reason to slow down or feel afraid."

The same principles of learning apply, and the same results of practice occur, when people learn emotional habits. For example, imagine yourself on the reservation in Tonto's moccasins when he suddenly looked down:

You probably would have felt afraid too; and without taking the time to think anything. Why? Because you would have been under the control of your fearful attitude (the unspoken form of your fearful beliefs) about the danger of stepping on rattlesnakes.

You learned your beliefs and attitudes about snakes the same way you learned your correct driving beliefs and attitudes—by practicing them. Now let's see how you did it.

If you are like most people, for as long as you remember, almost everything you have heard, read, thought, or pictured in your mind about rattlesnakes has been fearful; and you usually felt somewhat fearful most of the times you seriously thought about them. It didn't matter how slight that fearful feeling was; everytime you felt it, you were practicing it. And, even though you have never been threatened by a real rattlesnake, you have the same fear you would have had if you had been threatened in real life. That fact shows that mental practice is all you need to learn an emotional habit.

Don't misunderstand me though; I know it's perfectly healthy to have a rational fear of rattlesnakes. But the point I want to make is this: recent neurophysiologic research indicates that irrational emotional and physical habits can also result from mental practice alone. And this book shows that the irrational drinking habits that lead to alcoholism are largely caused by irrational mental practice. Understandably, therefore, the main therapeutic goal of the New Self-Help Alcoholic Treatment Method is to teach habitual problem drinkers how to recognize and get rid of their irrational, alcohol-related beliefs and attitudes. That simple act frees them to stop the habitual problem drinking that makes alcoholism unavoidable.

---

*This chapter plus Chapter 4 are available as one booklet: "The First Step In Solving A Drinking Problem", for $2.00 from The Rational Behavior Therapy (RBT) Center, College of Medicine, University of Kentucky, Lexington, Ky., 40506. Bulk prices available.

EMPHASIS QUESTIONS

1. Many people initially resist _____ that their _____ feelings are as simple as A, B, C.
2. Such people believe that if their emotions were as simple as A, B, C, they would have figured out their _____ ABC's for _____.
3. _____ focus is the main reason most people don't discover for _____ what causes their emotions.
4. When most people think about the cause of their emotions, they usually think only about the _____ world rather than about their _____.
5. Psychosomatic Fact #5 is: Almost all human emotions are as simple as ____, ____, ____.
6. Before you have an emotional reaction to anything, you first _____ something, then you think something, and finally you have a real, logical and correct _____ reaction.
7. When you react to an attitude you are really reacting to one of your unspoken beliefs. True or False?

8. There are two types of habitual emotions. Name them: _____ and _____ types.
9. People learn their emotional habits according to the same _____ steps they use when they _____ any habit.
10. If you can understand what happens when you learn how to _____ a car you understand all you need to _____ to understand how your _____ emotions work.
11. Most of the emotions you have every day are _____ emotions.
12. Beliefs are the _____ forms of your _____ and your attitudes are the _____ forms of your beliefs.
13. Beliefs and attitudes are cognitive or mental _____.
14. Your attitudes give you your so-called _____ emotional and physical reactions.
15. Beliefs are what free you from sub-human, animal-like dependence on the external world for your emotional and physical reactions. True or False?
16. You learned to be afraid of rattlesnakes by using the same ___, ___, ___ practice steps you used when you practiced _____ a car on the sofa in your _____.

CORRECT ANSWERS

1. accepting, emotional
2. emotional, themselves
3. wrong, themselves
4. external, thoughts
5. A, B, C
6. notice, emotional or emotive
7. True
8. A-C and B-C or attitudinal and belief
9. A, B, C, learn
10. drive, know, habitual
11. habitual
12. spoken, attitudes, unspoken
13. habits
14. spontaneous, or wordless
15. True
16. A, B, C, driving, home, or apartment or house

Why Thinking is More Important Than Emotional Feelings

The new Alcoholic Treatment Method involves problem drinkers as soon and as much as possible in helping themselves. At the end of the first treatment session, patients read the booklet entitled "The ABC's of Alcoholic Self-Help." The second session begins with a discussion of that material.

Dr. M.: Did you do the reading?
Bob: Yes, and there was one thing that really puzzled me.
Dr. M.: Oh, what was that?
Bob: Many of the things I read, I already knew were true. And what puzzles me is why I kept ignoring them; you know, the small things, like how I was thinking. I could see in advance that my drinking would get me in trouble, so why did I go ahead, knowing that trouble was coming?

THE COMMON MISTAKE PROBLEM DRINKERS MAKE

They believe their thinking is a small thing, too small to take seriously. But they almost always take seriously and act out their emotional feelings.

Problem drinkers are not the only people who make that mistake. **Most people do it,** especially when they feel emotionally distressed. But, their thoughts control almost everything they do. AND THAT FACT MAKES THINKING THE SINGLE MOST IMPORTANT HUMAN ACT.

Bad thinking is the main **cause of the bad emotional feelings** that people try to escape with alcohol and other legal and illegal drugs. Yet, people almost never seek help to improve their bad thinking. Instead, they almost always seek help to improve their bad feelings. And until they learn their emotional ABC's, they naively try to improve their bad emotional feelings without making a single change in their bad thoughts.

WHAT A HEALTHY BRAIN DOES
AND DOESN'T GUARANTEE

Your healthy brain DOES guarantee that your sincere thoughts will trigger the logical, correct emotional feelings for them. But, your healthy brain DOESN'T guarantee that your sincere thoughts will be rational or otherwise worth having.

Bob had already read "The ABC's of Alcoholic Self-Help." That made it easy for me to show him how his thinking had been (and still was) directing both his emotional and physical behavior.

Dr. M.: Well, your first mistake was in believing that your thinking was a small thing. The reality was and still is that your thinking is the most important thing you do. It controls you. No matter what legal or illegal things you voluntarily did or do, your thinking controlled and still controls that too.

Bob: But how can you say that? I used to think many times that if I didn't stop drinking, I was going to get into trouble; and that since I don't like being in trouble, I should stop drinking. But I kept right on drinking and getting into trouble. That's what puzzles me. Why did I do that?

Dr. M.: There's no mystery to it at all; your brain controls both your emotional and physical behavior; but because you control your brain with your beliefs and attitudes, that means that you are always in control of you. Don't you see that?

Bob: Yeah, I see it; that's why I don't see why I didn't follow my thinking and stay out of trouble.

WHY PEOPLE MISTRUST THEIR THOUGHTS

Thoughts are painless, easily changeable and ephemeral. Emotional feelings, however, often seem to hit like a ton of bricks; and equally as often emotional feelings tend to stay even after people want them to leave. Because emotional feelings can be intense and seemingly uncontrollable most people believe their emotions are more real and reliable than the seeming nothingness of their thoughts. And so most people logically, but naively ignore their thoughts in favor of their emotional feelings.

Ignoring your thoughts and acting on your emotional feelings is called GUT THINKING. It's fine when your feelings are rational; otherwise, it usually causes problems.

IT'S FOOLISH TO BLINDLY TRUST YOUR EMOTIONAL FEELINGS

A detailed look at a common example of such blind trust will show you why. People who worry more than they want to often say, "I worry about every bad thing I can think of; I know it's a silly thing to do; but every time I tell myself not to worry, my gut tells me I'm wrong, that I really should worry—so I worry."

That's the typical logic of people who blindly trust their gut (i.e., their emotional) feelings. That's a foolish habit because emotional feelings are triggered either by beliefs (i.e., sincere spoken thoughts) or by attitudes (i.e., sincere unspoken thoughts. (See chapter five).

Before people in the above example learn the ABC's of their habitual emotions, they don't realize that it's their attitude ("I should worry") that makes their gut seem to say that they really should worry. Such gut thinking (as opposed to brain thinking) is irrational for two reasons.

First, it makes people afraid to stop irrational worry.

Second, irrational worry often leads people to take irrational physical actions.

USEFUL INSIGHTS INTO GUT THINKING

Gut thinking can be both safe and useful, if your emotional feelings are rational and you know your emotional ABC's. Otherwise, gut thinking is a dangerously foolish way to control yourself.

Next I used the ABC model of human emotions to get Bob to see that he had been following his thinking all along, even when it got him into trouble.

Dr. M.: But you did follow your thinking. Granted, it was your alcohol-induced, gut thinking rather than your sober brain thinking; that's why you got into trouble. BUT! It was still you following your thinking.

Bob: I don't see how you can say that. I knew stealing is wrong, but I did it anyway.

Dr. M.: Tell me, when you were sober and saw a check in someone's mailbox, and thought: "Boy, I sure could use that money; I could pay some of my bills, and . . ."

Bob: Buy me a fifth. (laughter)

Dr. M.: Yes, buy you a fifth. But did you just walk right over and steal the check?

Bob: When I was sober?

Dr. M.: Yes.

Bob: No, I'd see that it was a stupid idea, and I would put it out of my mind and go on about my business.

Dr. M.: In other words, when you were sober, you'd feel afraid of getting caught and going to jail, so you would dismiss the idea of stealing.

Bob: Right.

Dr. M.: But what if you later thought: "Maybe I could get away with it?"

Bob: If I hadn't been drinking, I would still chicken out and not do it.

Dr. M.: All right, that's my point. When you were sober and thought about stealing, you would feel the usual law-abiding citizen's fear of going to jail, and you would put the thought out of your mind, right?

Bob: Right, that's why I can't understand why I would end up doing it anyway. You think maybe I really wanted to get in trouble?

Dr. M.: Well, you tell me. Did you really want to go to jail?

Bob: I don't think so, but a court psychologist told me that once. He said I unconsciously wanted to punish myself.

Dr. M.: I don't see any reason to believe that. I think it's much more likely that you didn't want to go to jail; but after you had had a few drinks, the alcohol prevented you from feeling afraid of going to jail. And when people don't feel afraid while thinking about doing something they want to do, their positive, wanting thoughts trigger positive feeling of hope. That's what happened to you. When you thought about stealing after having had a few drinks, instead of feeling afraid, you felt hopeful. That's what you called, in first session, "feeling that I could do things that I couldn't do when I was sober." So, the more you drank and thought about stealing, the more IRRATIONALLY confident of success you became and the better you felt about the idea of stealing; and sooner or later...

Bob: I ended up doing it.

Dr. M.: Right! After alcohol eliminated your law-abiding fear, you changed your thinking from "I might get caught" to "I won't get caught."

Bob: Yeah, I see what you mean. Alcohol does that to me. That's why I need to give it up, so I can stay out of trouble.

Dr. M.: I agree. But the point I want you to see here is that you were still doing it. You can't act on thoughts that you DON'T have at the present moment. That's why you have to be thinking honest thoughts NOW! if you are going to behave honestly NOW! Do you understand what I'm saying?

Bob: Yeah. When I'm drinking, I don't feel scared of getting caught, so I think I won't get caught. So I steal.

Dr. M.: Right! The two main reasons people repeatedly do anything are: they hope to get something they want, consciously want; it's NOT unconscious at all. And the other reason is they are consciously afraid of getting something they consciously want to AVOID. But alcohol makes it easy to replace rational fear with irrational hope; and it makes you feel good and right about doing it. Unfortunately, though, irrational hope doesn't change objective reality; so you got caught.

Bob: And if I keep on drinking, I'm going to keep on stealing and getting into trouble. Is that what you are saying?

Dr. M.: It sure seems that way.

At that point Bob seemed to understand that it was his alcoholic thinking that kept getting him into trouble, but it was still his thinking. He also seemed to understand why he would have to stop drinking in order to stay out of trouble. My job then was to show Bob why he could stop drinking now, even though he had not done it before.

Dr. M.: You see, before now you had never learned your emotional ABC's. So you didn't see that you were creating the negative emotions you kept trying to drown with alcohol. And because you didn't know how to make yourself feel better without drinking, you always had a logical reason to drink. And because alcohol also let you feel irrationally hopeful about getting away with things you were afraid to do when you were sober, you began to think alcohol made your brain work better. For example, when you got out of jail on bond that first time what did you do?

Next I tried to get Bob to see how absurd it was to think that alcohol made his brain work better.

Dr. M.: You also said drinking made you express yourself better. But tell me, have you ever talked to people when they were high on alcohol and you were still sober?
Bob: Yeah.
Dr. M.: Well, did they express themselves better or worse than you did?
Bob: (Smiling) I see what you mean.
Dr. M.: Okay, so it wasn't that you expressed youself better after drinking. It was just that you were no longer afraid to talk; so you talked, even though many times you probably didn't always make too much sense.
Bob: I see what you mean.

Dr. M.: And you have always gone back to drinking because you have never learned how to feel emotionally satisfied without alcohol. So, the solution to your drinking problem is quite simple. All you have to do is learn to feel emotionally satisfied with yourself with sober thinking, instead of with problem drinking. Then you will be free to pursue your life in a sober, law-abiding way.

Bob: That's what I want to do.

Dr. M.: Well, the best way to do it is to make sure all your sober thinking is rational. Rational thinking causes rational emotions, and rational emotions prevent problem drinking. So, before your next sessions read this little booklet entitled "The Rational Use of Your Emotional ABC's." It tells you the big difference between really rational thinking and the believable but irrational kind you have been using.*

EMPHASIS QUESTIONS

1. A common mistake problem drinkers make is they _____ their thinking in favor of their emotional _____.
2. Most emotionally distressed people question their personal beliefs before acting on them. True or False?
3. Bob was stealing because he did not know stealing was wrong. True or False?
4. Bob got arrested because he was following his thinking. True or False?
5. When Bob was drinking he became irrationally confident of success at stealing because he didn't feel _____ of getting caught.
6. Alcohol led Bob to believe that he could do things when he drank that he _____ do when he was _____.
7. To stay out of trouble Bob had to stop _____.
8. Bob didn't see that he was _____ the emotional pain he tried to _____ with alcohol.

---

*The Rational Use of Your Emotional ABC's is the next Chapter of this book.

9. Bob didn't see that he was creating his emotional pain because he needed glasses. True or False?
10. Bob probably didn't really express himself better after drinking. True or False?
11. Bob went back to drinking because he never learned how to feel _____ _____ without alcohol.
12. To start feeling better without alcohol, Bob first had to learn his _____ ABC's.
13. A good way that Bob could have kept from drinking was to have made sure his sober thinking was _____.
14. Rational thinking causes rational _____; rational emotions _____ problem drinking.

CORRECT ANSWERS

1. ignore, feelings
2. False
3. False
4. True
5. afraid
6. couldn't, sober
7. drinking
8. creating, causing or triggering, drown
9. False
10. True
11. emotionally satisfied, or, as good, or happy enough
12. emotional
13. rational
14. emotions, prevent

7

The Rational Use of Your Emotional ABC's

Your emotional ABC's tell you the three parts of your emotions. They also show you why and how you can change your emotions almost at will, without alcohol or other drugs. But your ABC's don't tell you whether or not it's in your best interest to change your emotions. You have to decide that for yourself. Before you try to make that important decision, it's best to clearly understand the next two important facts.

WHAT YOUR EMOTIONS DO

First, they give you your three different types of emotive feelings.

Second, each specific positive, negative, or neutral emotion makes you more likely to react physically in that specific way than in either of the other two ways. For example, when you feel angry you are more likely to behave angrily than you are to behave calmly or happily.

80

Keep in mind that I'm only talking about what you are more likely to do. As you well know, from having done it many times, you can act against your emotions. For example, most people at one time or another have behaved calmly or even pleasantly while feeling as angry as the devil.

WHAT ABOUT ACTING AGAINST YOUR EMOTIONS?

First off, **it takes more conscious effort** than it does to act them out. In addition, in spite of your greater effort, when you act against your negative emotions, **your results can still be as unsatisfactory** as they might have been if you had gone ahead and acted out your emotions.

Essentially the same situation exists with your neutral and positive emotions. Usually, though, the intensity of those emotional feelings is much less than the intensity of your negative ones.

And you are much less likely to have significant emotional problems because of your neutral or positive emotions than you are because of your negative ones. Almost always it's negative emotions that get you in trouble, cause you to abuse alcohol and other drugs, as well as cause you to get psychotherapy. Because of those facts many people wonder:

ARE NEGATIVE EMOTIONS HEALTHY REACTIONS?

Because I'm a psychiatrist I can answer that question without fear of valid contradiction. Of course negative emotions are **healthy reactions.** They are both as healthy and useful as either positive or neutral emotions. But with all three types of emotional reactions:

HOW MUCH CAN BE MUCH MORE IMPORTANT THAN WHAT TYPE

Too much or too little of almost any habitual behavior can be unhealthy. For example, you can get sick and even die from habitually overeating; and you can get sick and even die from habitually undereating. But, in either case, you can end up being just as dead.

The situation is quite similar for your positive, negative, and neutral emotions. Too little or too much of any one of them can indicate serious emotional disturbance. So, with your physical as well as with your emotional health, the quantity of your behavior can be much more important than the type of it.

MENTALLY AND EMOTIONALLY HEALTHY BEHAVIORS

Such behaviors usually have these two features: **They are based on objective facts;** and when you maintain them, **they protect or improve your mental and emotional health.** Such behaviors are called rational behaviors; **and the thinking that makes them possible is called rational thinking.**

WHAT IS RATIONAL THINKING?

First, let me tell you what it isn't. It ISN'T WHAT MOST PEOPLE BELIEVE IT IS. Most people believe that rational thinking is the kind they already do; and they believe that irrational thinking is the kind you do when you disagree with them. That's understandable; sane people don't go around sincerely thinking thoughts they believe are irrational. In reality, though, what most people call rational and irrational thinking usually turns out to be merely personal beliefs and differences of opinions, both of which often prove to be irrational. Obviously, therefore, you need more than just your personal beliefs and disagreements to recognize and separate rational thinking from the irrational kind. That's why in Rational Self-Counseling you use a relatively objective set of rules for recognizing rational behaviors.

Rational Rule #1
RATIONAL THINKING IS BASED ON OBVIOUS FACTS

Be careful when you try to use this rule. Remember, truth does not have to be fact.

The New Self-Help Treatment approach is based on the fact that to the extent problem drinkers can learn anything, they can learn the facts about helping themselves to happiness with Rational Self-Counseling. Obviously, though, none of them has to learn those facts; and every day millions of them simply refuse to do so. Instead, they rely on truths. They do that because they haven't yet made the following important insight.

Rational Insight #1
EVEN THOUGH BELIEFS ARE ALWAYS TRUTHS FOR THE BELIEVERS, TRUTHS OFTEN HAVE LITTLE TO DO WITH OBVIOUS FACTS

The next illustrations give you common examples of thinking that disobeys the first rule for rational thinking and thinking that obeys it. Notice how easily Rational Rule #1 helps you to separate the one type of thinking from the other.

Truthful Thinking	Factual Thinking

When people's beliefs are irrational, their thinking will be truthful, but still irrational and often self-defeating.	When people keep their thinking factual, their beliefs are most likely to be rational and helpful to them.

Rational Rule #2
RATIONAL THINKING HELPS YOU PROTECT YOURSELF FROM PROBABLE HARM

No one chooses to be born; but, as long as you act to avoid death, you are choosing to live. Making the choice to live immediately gives you two other unavoidable choices:

(1) The choice to live as self-destructively as possible.

OR

(2) The choice to live as self-protectively as possible.

That fact brings me to Rational Insight #2.

Rational Insight #2
RATIONAL THINKING IS PRIMARILY FOR PEOPLE WHO CHOOSE TO LIVE AS SELF-PROTECTIVELY AS POSSIBLE

The next illustrations demonstrate the big difference between self-destructive thinking and self-protective thinking.

Self-Destructive Thinking   **Self-Protective Thinking**

Right doesn't always win. In fact you can be dead right, but still end up being just plain dead.

Rational Rule #3
RATIONAL THINKING HELPS YOU EFFICIENTLY ACHIEVE YOUR SHORT- AND LONG-TERM GOALS

When you are most honest with yourself, you see that you happily do things mainly for one reason—you hope to get something you want. That's a fact, even though all you hope for is the good feelings you usually have about voluntarily helping someone.

Now consider this fact for a moment: **unless you kill yourself** today, you will probably be alive tomorrow. Would it not be better, therefore, if you have and act on HOPES today that will not interfere with achieving your HOPES for tomorrow? And would it not be best of all if achieving your HOPES for today helps you achieve your HOPES for tomorrow? If you don't agree with those ideas, then rational thinking may not be the best kind for you.

To quickly check out that possibility, keep an open mind and carefully study the next illustrations. Afterwards, decide which type of thinking would probably produce the greatest short and long-term payoffs for you.

| Short-Term Thinking | Short- and Long-Term Thinking |

Most problems with job pressure are imaginary. That's why The Emotional ABC's plus Rational Rule #3 quickly solve them.

Rational Rule #4
RATIONAL THINKING HELPS YOU PREVENT SIGNIFICANT CONFLICT WITH OTHER PEOPLE—YOUR PARENTS, LOVED ONES, BOSSES, POLICE, ET CETERA

Significant conflict is the amount you don't want to have; it doesn't help you; and you act to avoid it. The next illustrations show how quickly irrational thinking can lead you to significant conflict with others, and how easily rational thinking helps you avoid it.

Conflict Producing Thoughts	Conflict Preventing Thoughts

Irrational thinking is the main direct cause of irrational drinking. In addition, they reinforce each other. That's why they stay together.	Rational thinking is the main direct cause of rational drinking. In addition they reinforce each other. That's why they stay together.

AN IMPORTANT FACT TO REMEMBER:

WHETHER OR NOT YOU HAVE BEEN DRINKING, IT IS STILL YOUR THINKING THAT TRIGGERS AND CONTROLS YOUR BEHAVIOR.

Rational Rule #5
RATIONAL THINKING HELPS YOU HABITUALLY FEEL THE EMOTIONS YOU WANT TO FEEL

The next illustrations demonstrate how easily sincere but irrational thinking makes people feel miserable in the same situation where sincere rational thinking makes them feel good.

Unwanted Pain-Producing Thoughts	Pain-Preventing Thoughts

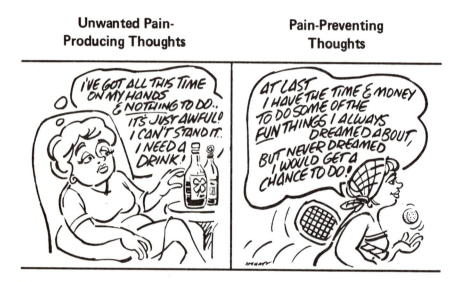

Like millions of people, Mrs. Green had the popular belief that her family was more important to her than she was to herself. That belief caused her to structure her life around serving her family. That fact made her joy in living dependent upon having a family to serve, and how well she served it.

If she had known her Emotional ABC's and the Five Rules For Rational Thinking, she would have realized that her joy in life depended only on what she believed about what she did, instead of the fact that she did it. Then she would have rationally included serving her family in the structure of her life. And she still would have served her family just as well, if not better. In addition, she would have made a quicker, more rational adjustment when her family decided to serve itself.

Rational Insight #3
AFTER ENOUGH PRACTICE YOUR RATIONAL THINKING LETS YOU REFUSE TO FEEL ANY WORSE EMOTIONALLY THAN YOU WANT TO FEEL

Because repetition is the royal road to rapid learning, let's quickly review the five rules for rational thinking.

THE FIVE RULES FOR RATIONAL THINKING

RR#1 Rational thinking is based on obvious facts.
RR#2 Rational thinking helps you protect yourself from probable harm.
RR#3 Rational thinking helps you efficiently achieve your short- and long-term goals.
RR#4 Rational thinking helps you prevent significant conflict with other people—your parents, loved ones, bosses, police, et cetera.
RR#5 Rational thinking helps you habitually feel the emotions you want to feel.

At this point many people wonder:

The correct answer is "yes"; but nobody is perfect. **Your thoughts, feelings, and actions won't obey all five of the rational rules all of the time.**

For example, sometimes you can't know what the objective facts are. And sometimes one or more of the rules will be irrelevant to your situation. **That's why thoughts, feelings, and actions can be called rational if they just obey at least three of the five rules.** When they obey more than three of the five rules, THAT'S GREAT!! You will have that much more rational protection; still, it's sometimes useful to know that you won't always need it.

The correct answer is "no"; it's really easy. All you have to do is honestly answer:

THE FIVE QUESTIONS FOR RATIONAL THINKING

1. Is my thinking here factual? (RR#1)
2. Will my thinking here help me to protect myself from probable harm? (RR#2)

3. Will my thinking here help me efficiently achieve my short- and long-term goals? (RR#3)

4. Will my thinking here help me avoid significant conflict with others? (RR#4)

5. Will my thinking here help me habitually feel the emotions I want to feel? (RR#5)

Honest "NO's" for any three of those questions clearly reveal irrational thinking.

Since most people learn best by doing, I'll let you take a few minutes now to practice using the five questions for rational thinking. Imagine that you are Alice, the person in the next illustration. The five questions for rational thinking follow the illustration. Answer each question either "YES", "NO", or "DNA" (for "Does Not Apply"). Then decide whether or not you agree with Alice's conclusion.

REMEMBER, you must have at least three "Yes's" for your thinking to be rational.

After Alice gives you her conclusions, I will explain why she was correct.

To get the most from this exercise, **repress the urge to cheat.** Actually answer the five questions for yourself; then reach your own conclusion before you read Alice's.

A. "I don't like the way he seems to talk down his nose to me. But I refuse to upset myself about his ill manners."

1.	Is my thinking here factual?	YES	NO	DNA
2.	Will my thinking here help me to protect myself from probable harm?	YES	NO	DNA
3.	Will my thinking here help me efficiently achieve my short- and long-term goals?	YES	NO	DNA
4.	Will my thinking here help me avoid significant conflict with others?	YES	NO	DNA
5.	Will my thinking here help me habitually feel the emotions I want to feel?	YES	NO	DNA

Therefore, my thinking here is _____.(Fill in what you think Alice said).

Before you compare my explanation to yours, remember: what's rational for one person may not be rational for another person. Therefore, your ideas can be different from mine and still be rational for you. The only important question is: "For me in that situation, would my ideas merit at least three HONEST Yes answers to the five questions for rational thinking?" If they would, your ideas would be rational for you, even though they might not be rational for someone else.

Alice answered "Yes" to questions 1, 3, 4, and 5. Therefore, her thinking was rational. It was a fact that Mr. Black didn't talk to her the way she wanted him to talk; but Alice saw no rational reason to upset herself just because some people didn't act the way she wanted them to act.

Most people make that insight soon after they accept the following obvious facts:

(1) You can't control the way other people behave.
(2) It's a foolish waste of time to upset yourself about something you can't control.
(3) You always control your mind; that fact puts you in

direct control of you and your emotions.
(4) You are usually better off when you control your emotions to your satisfaction.

Alice clearly saw that all she would get for being upset with Mr. Black was more upset. Since she knew she wouldn't like that feeling, she rationally refused to upset herself any more than she wanted to be in that situation.

EMPHASIS QUESTIONS

1. Rational thinking is primarily for people who choose to live as _____ as possible.
2. It really is _____ to be rational about _____.
3. Rational thinking is based on _____ facts.
4. Rational thinking helps you protect yourself from probable _____.
5. Rational thinking helps you prevent significant _____ with other people.
6. Rational thinking helps you habitually _____ the _____ you want to _____.
7. Significant conflict is the _____ you dislike enough to _____ to _____.
8. Sincere irrational thinking can make people feel miserable in the same situation where sincere rational thinking makes them feel good. True or False?
9. The five rules for Rational Thinking are also the five rules for Rational _____ and Rational _____ actions.
10. Your thoughts, feelings, and actions are called "rational" if they obey at least _____ of the five rules.

PLEASE NOTE

This chapter is available as a booklet: "Rational Thinking Stops Irrational Drinking", for $1.50 from The RBT Center, College of Medicine, University of Kentucky, Lexington, Ky., 40506. Bulk prices available.

CORRECT ANSWERS

1. self-protectively
2. easy, yourself
3. obvious
4. harm
5. conflict
6. feel, emotions, feel
7. amount, act, avoid
8. True
9. Emotions, Physical
10. three

Wanting Versus Craving a Drink

Chapter six gave you a typical example of the disadvantage of blindly trusting your emotional feelings. But what about the people who say they have tried changing their thoughts, but their feelings still didn't change. For example, every day thousands of students say: "I just can't speak in class; it's too threatening. I get scared to death. Now I know that's silly. Nobody has ever died from just standing up in a class and answering a professor's question; and I've actually told myself that; but thinking it just doesn't help me. My guts tell me I'm lying. I really do feel something terrible might happen; it's just too frightening."

The problem there is emotional ignorance. Those people don't realize that it's their fearful attitude (i.e., their unspoken but sincere belief that something terrible probably will happen if they speak up) that triggers their fear. Once they recognize their unspoken belief and start acting against it, they quickly stop being afraid and begin to speak up in class.

No, they didn't try that; what they tried was impossible; that's why they failed. They tried to trick themselves into having different types of emotions without having different types of thoughts. To see that fact clearly, look objectively at the thoughts they had.

Potentially Frightening Thoughts

(1) It's too threatening.
(2) I get scared to death.
(3) But thinking that doesn't help me.
(4) My guts tell me I'm lying.
(5) I really do feel something terrible might happen.
(6) It's just too frightening.

Potentially Calming Thoughts

(1) I know that's silly.
(2) Nobody ever died from it.

For each potentially calming thought, they had three potentially frightening ones. In addition they let their guts completely overrule their two potentially calming thoughts. Consequently, there was no objective change in the quality of their moment-to-moment beliefs. Understandably, therefore, they ended up believing "I just can't speak in class; it's just too threatening."

Sincere, moment-to-moment beliefs direct and control moment-to-moment emotions. And people cannot change those emotions if they use them to veto or cancel new ideas. To get new emotional feelings in old situations people must base their moment-to-moment beliefs on facts rather than on their emotional feelings.

What does all that have to do with helping cured alcoholics stay dry? A whole lot! Confusing **wanting** alcoholic drinks with **craving** them is one of the most common reasons cured alcoholics jump off the wagon.

Once cured alcoholics and other problem drinkers learn to act on the facts about craving, wanting, desiring, and needing, they are more likely to stay on the wagon.

PRIMARY CRAVING AND DRINKING

Primary craving is an intense, unavoidable, involuntary, negative urge to ingest an addictive drug. Primary craving occurs only in the second stage of drug addiction; and it starts automatically after an addicted body loses enough of the drug to disturb the body's physiologic homeostasis. The greater the loss of the drug, the more severe and powerful the primary craving becomes, until addicts do one of these three things:

1. Ingest enough of the addictive drug or a substitute drug to stop the craving and restore drug-induced physiologic homeostasis.
OR
2. Go "COLD TURKEY", that is, go through withdrawal from the addictive drug without a substitute drug.
OR
3. Get medically detoxified and establish healthy physiologic homeostasis without the addictive drug.

WHY MOST ALCOHOLICS USUALLY CHOOSE ALCOHOL

To get medically detoxified usually requires the time, effort, and hassle of going to a hospital or jail. Until alcoholics get absolutely helpless, they can usually get a few drinks much quicker and with much less hassle than they can get into a hospital or jail.

Going Cold Turkey Works, BUT!

It is the most frightening, painful, and dangerous way to reestablish healthy physiologic homeostasis. Up to 25 percent of alcoholics who go "cold turkey" DIE in the process. Understandably, therefore, most alcoholics choose alcohol.

SECONDARY CRAVING AND JUMPING OFF THE WAGON

Secondary craving feels very similar to early primary craving; but the similarity ends there. Primary craving is an addicted body's physiologic distress scream. Secondary craving is merely a learned urge to ingest an addictive drug in situations associated with past ingestion.

For example, take problem drinkers who habitually got drunk in bars or to ease negative emotions; they can sober up, and honestly NOT WANT to drink; yet when they go in or even pass by bars, or get angry, depressed, etc., those past cues for drinking trigger secondary craving for alcoholic drinks.

Unfortunately, most alcoholic treatment programs neglect to teach alcoholics the difference between harmless secondary craving and the early stage of their old, more dangerous primary craving. Consequently, when cured alcoholics get intense but harmless secondary cravings, they often get fearfully confused and disgusted at themselves. They had been convinced that their last treatment had cured them; now they think it didn't. Then it's just a matter of time before they give up and jump off the wagon again, even though they really never intended to do so.

Such giving up comes largely from the incorrect belief that being cured means never craving alcohol again. In the sterile alcohol-free setting of most treatment programs cured (dry) alcoholics either don't crave or they crave very little. Understandably, therefore, most of them decide: "This time I have really been cured." So they leave their treatment programs sincerely expecting never to crave alcohol or to get sick (i.e., be alcoholic) again. But their naive expectations don't change the facts.

THE MYTH OF DRY DT'S

In the real world of alcohol at almost every turn, most cured alcoholics quickly come face to face with many past cues for drinking and craving alcohol—restaurants, bars, parties, intense negative emotional states, etc. Predictably, those old cues trigger secondary alcoholic craving. The confused alcoholics think, "Damn! I've been fooling myself. I thought I was really cured! After all the hassles I've had with alcohol and trying to get well!! Now, here I am still wanting to drink again. I really must be some kind of drunken nut. I'm even worse off than A LOUSY SKID-ROW BUM! At least they want to drink themselves to death! My God! How could I have sunk so low?"

Such self-denigrating thoughts trigger strong negative emotions; those negative emotions intensify the total discomfort and the secondary craving for alcohol. That makes those harmless cravings seem even more like the potentially dangerous primary ones. That's when sober alcoholics panic: "My God!" they think, "I'm having dry DT's. I need a drink. I've just got to have a drink."

Sincere thoughts of NEED or GOT TO HAVE are the strongest human motivators for immediate action. Understandably, therefore, these confused but cured alcoholics begin to drink; and predictably, they quickly feel relieved. Then they conclude: "Well, I may as well go on and enjoy myself until I have to go in for treatment again. Maybe the next time the doctors will give me a triple dose of treatment and really cure me."

To help cured alcoholics avoid that self-defeating end, we teach them the following, relatively objective way to recognize and separate their cravings from their wishes and wants, and all three from their hopes and desires, and all of these from their needs.

WISHES AND WANTS*

Your wishes and wants are merely perceptions and thoughts that you would be better off if you were to get what you want or wish for. Because wishes and wants are merely thoughts, they exist only in your mind. That's why you can change them instantly and at will.

You usually WISH for events that cannot or probably will not happen. You usually WANT events that could happen, but you are either unwilling to do or you cannot do what's necessary to make those events happen. That's why your wishes and wants do NOT usually motivate you to sustained achieving action.

You may wish to wake up a billionaire. You certainly want the airplanes you ride in to land safely. But you usually can't make either event happen, so you don't usually try to do anything about either of them.

HOPES AND DESIRES

Hopes and desires are A-B-C type emotions. They consist of perceived objects at A, ideas of want at B, plus positive urges at C to get the wanted objects at A.

UNLIKE wishes and wants, HOPES pleasantly motivate you for sustained, achieving action. The continuous hope of early problem drinkers to feel better with alcohol is their main motivation for the habitual alcohol abuse that creates their drinking problems.

---

*Webster's Dictionary may not (probably does not) agree with any of this. But then, Webster doesn't treat problem drinkers. I recommend this increased precision, though, only because it has proven to be useful in helping problem drinkers understand and solve their drinking problems.

DESIRES are relatively intense, but pleasantly impelling, forms of hopes. For example, you can hope to drink cold beer at your party next week without desiring to drink now. But your hope will motivate you to go buy beer sometime before the party.*

Suppose, however, you forget to put the beer in the refrigerator; at party time the beer will be hot. Therefore, you probably would not desire (i.e., want plus have an urge) to drink that beer. But you might well desire to drink the cold beer someone else brings to the party. Still, you would not crave that beer unless you have a drinking problem.

THE RATIONAL VIEW OF NEEDS

Rational Self-Counseling teaches people to recognize two kinds of NEEDS, or essentials, for being: OBJECTIVE NEEDS and SUBJECTIVE NEEDS.

An OBJECTIVE NEED exists independently of human wants, desires or demands. To be alive people need (i.e., HAVE GOT TO or MUST HAVE) food, water, and protection from life-threatening events. To be happy, sad or calm healthy people need (i.e., HAVE GOT TO or MUST HAVE) happy, sad or calm beliefs and attitudes. Those are physiologic and psychophysiologic facts. They exist whether or not people know about them, believe them or deny them. OBJECTIVE NEEDS are the only ones rationally thinking people are concerned about.

A SUBJECTIVE NEED exists ONLY in the minds of people. It consists of a want for something PLUS a self-imposed personal punishment for not getting it. For example, many people believe they need love or approval from certain other people to be satisfied with themselves. In reality, such people merely want that love or approval; but when they don't get it, they make themselves miserable (i.e., punish themselves).

Many habitual problem drinkers believe they need (i.e., have got to have) alcoholic drinks to feel better emotionally. In reality,

---

*If you merely wish or want beer at your party, you might just wait and see if someone happens to bring some.

they merely want alcohol-induced emotional feelings; but they irrationally make themselves miserable (i.e., punish themselves) if they don't drink. Then they drink, get relief, and conclude that their relief proved they needed to drink to feel better.

Because subjective needs exist only in people's minds, people always have two possibilities for increased emotional comfort:

1. They can get what they want.

OR

2. They can change their minds and stop punishing themselves.

Often people can't get what they want; but they ALWAYS CAN change their minds. Problem drinkers need to remember that fact to avoid confusion.

A FOUR POINT SUMMARY

1. WISHES and WANTS for alcohol are merely perceptions and ideas, existing only in people's minds. That's why problem drinkers can instantly stop or start wishing for or wanting for alcohol. All they have to do is change their minds.
2. HOPES and DESIRES for alcohol are A-B-C type emotions. They consist of perceptions, ideas of want plus positive emotive urges to get what's wanted. Hopes and desires can usually be stopped or started as quickly and in the same way as any other emotion.
3. PRIMARY ALCOHOLIC CRAVING is unavoidable, chemically induced, physical distress. It's caused largely by loss of alcohol from an alcoholically addicted body. Primary alcoholic craving can be both painful and life threatening. But primary alcoholic craving can be stopped relatively quickly by ingesting more alcohol and permanently by either:
    a. Medical detoxification
    or
    b. "Cold Turkey" withdrawal.
4. SECONDARY ALCOHOLIC CRAVING is a learned A-C or B-C type habitual emotional reaction to situations or memories associated with repeated past problem drinking.

Secondary alcoholic craving occurs involuntarily on cue, even though the problem drinker DOESN'T WANT to drink alcoholic drinks.

Though secondary alcoholic cravings are unpleasant, they are neither harmful nor over-powering. Secondary alcoholic cravings are habitual emotional reactions. That's why they can usually be started or stopped as quickly, and in the same way, as any other habitual emotional reactions. And just like all habits, to stop secondary alcoholic craving permanently, sober problem drinkers must practice habit extinction.

A COMMON QUESTION:

No, but if you want to help problem drinkers help themselves most quickly, such precision is useful. The sincere thought "I want it" is probably the single most popular, self-motivating idea people have; and the sincere thought "I've just got to have it" is probably the single most POWERFUL self-motivating idea people have.

When people (particularly problem drinkers) believe they can't get the things they want or "just have to have," they begin to think life is not worth living. Such logic is probably the single most important reason there are revolutionaries ("Give me liberty or give me death"), martyrs, and terrorists.

In moderately intense form the irrational beliefs "I've just got to, but I can't" are the two most common mental cues for simple depressions in everyday life. Trying to control such depressions with alcohol is one of the main reasons people become habitual problem drinkers.

TABLE OF LEARNED AND NON-LEARNED URGES TO DRINK

LEARNED URGES

Wants and Wishes Manifested By:	Desires and Hopes Manifested By:
A. A perception	A. A perception
B. Passive nonachieving ideas	B. Activating achieving ideas
C. No significant emotive or physical reactions	C. Logical emotive and physical reactions

Secondary Cravings

A. A perception and		B. Thought, mental images and
C. Logical emotive and physical reactions	OR	C. Logical emotive and physical reactions

*NONLEARNED URGES**
(Drug induced)

Primary Cravings Result From

A. Internal loss of addictive drugs	Plus	C. Logical emotive or physiologic disturbance caused by A

---

*This Chapter is available in booklet for $1.50 from the RBT Center, College of Medicine, University of Kentucky, Lexington, Kentucky 40506. Bulk price available.

EMPHASIS QUESTIONS

1. Wishes and _____ are manifested by A. _____, and B. _____ ideas about having what's wished for or wanted.
2. _____ and desires are manifested by A. perceptions, B. _____ ideas, and C. logical _____ and _____ reactions.
3. Needs and _____ cravings are manifested by _____ emotive _____.
4. The first step in getting rid of a drug habit is to create and maintain a sincere desire to get rid of it. True or False?
5. To desire something you must _____ it plus have a logical achieving _____ that leads to _____ action.
6. After alcoholics give up the idea of drinking, they can still experience secondary cravings. True or False?
7. Dr. Maultsby said that when he learned to smoke, all he needed to keep him diligently practicing were his irrationally _____ thoughts of himself as a _____ kid plus irrationally positive thoughts of himself as a _____ man.
8. When your body is physically addicted to drugs, you have to keep using them to feel physically comfortable. True or False?
9. In Rational Self-Counseling there is no difference between wanting and craving. True or False?
10. Wishes and wants are _____: they exist only in your _____.
11. Hopes and desires are positive _____: they motivate people to _____ actions.
12. Addicts have no control over their _____ craves.
13. Problem drinkers usually want to drink if they take a drink. True or False?
14. Problem drinkers often sincerely want to stop drinking, but their secondary cravings influence them to change their non-drinking thinking to drinking thinking. True or False?
15. If problem drinkers really are sincere in their resolution to stop drinking, they won't crave alcohol anymore. True or False?
16. Problem drinkers are quite likely to "jump off" the wagon if they naively believe their sincere intention to stop drinking will prevent future _____ _____.

CORRECT ANSWERS

1. wants. perception, passive
2. Hopes, active, urges, achieving
3. primary, disturbed, reactions
4. True
5. want, urges, acquiring
6. True
7. negative, non-smoking, smoking
8. True
9. False
10. ideas, mind
11. emotions, sustained or acquiring or productive
12. primary
13. False
14. True
15. False
16. alcoholic craves

Teaching Cured Alcoholics About Alcohol Addiction and De-Addiction

Chapter two showed you how and why habitual problem drinkers accidentally make themselves alcoholics. The New Self-Help Treatment Method teaches cured alcoholics the details of their accident plus how to avoid it in the future (chapters 10, 11, 12, 13 and 14). Such cured alcoholics are most likely to stay there and be happy.

Rarely do alcoholics know it, but most addictive processes are essentially the same. That fact makes **stopping habitual problem drinking as simple as stopping habitual smoking.** That's why I use the example of cigarette addiction to teach alcoholics about de-addicting themselves from alcohol. Most alcoholics are either addicted to cigarettes or they know it's possible to get permanently de-addicted from them.

Bob's initial reaction to my routine was typical.

"Are you trying to tell me that my alcohol habit is as simple as my smoking habit?"

Dr. M.: That is right. It's as simple as your cigarette addiction.
Bob: That is hard to believe.

Dr. M.: Not really. Alcohol just seems more complex because cigarettes haven't caused you as much trouble as alcohol has.

Bob: That's true.

Dr. M.: And you are probably convinced that you could stop smoking if you really wanted to, but you are equally convinced that you can't stop drinking. So it's understandable why the two habits seem to you to be different, even though they are essentially the same.

Bob: Now that; Uh! I don't see that at all.

Dr. M.: Okay, what's the main first sign of any addiction? It's mental dependence: the sincere, but irrational belief that you can't be satisfied without the drug. And habitually acting on that belief makes you physically dependent and a compulsive user; that's the second stage of addiction. And then the main thing is the powerful urge to use the drug called PRIMARY CRAVING. Those two stages are the same regardless of whether the drug is tobacco or alcohol. "Primary craving" implies that there is secondary craving; and there is, and alcoholics need to know the big difference between the two, so they can keep from getting confused and jumping off the wagon.

Bob: Why is that?

Dr. M.: Because secondary craving feels like the early stage of primary craving. But in reality it's nothing more than a harmless A-C or B-C type emotional reaction, triggered by old drinking cues, such as bars, parties, or just daydreaming about drinking like you did in prison. Then there are the emotional drinking cues, such as being angry, anxious, depressed, or even being happy, like after getting a raise or winning a prize and wanting to celebrate. After you are addicted, even though you honestly don't want to drink any more, any of those old drinking cues can and will trigger secondary craving for alcoholic drinks, even months after your last drink. Do you follow me?

Bob: I think so. I mean, I understand your words, but I'm not sure I know what you mean.

Dr. M.: Don't worry about it. When you hear it again on your tape, you will not only understand it better, you will see how it applies to you. It just sounds complex now because it is a new way of thinking to you. But if you just keep in mind that problem drinking is as simple as habitual smoking, the rest will be easy.

THE USE OF TAPE RECORDER IN RSC

Most permanent behavior change is really behavioral re-education. Simple repetition is one of the fastest roads to rapid learning; that's why I routinely tape record my counseling sessions. Later my patients listen to their recordings. That simple maneuver greatly intensifies therapeutic learning. In addition to listening repeatedly to the tapes of their own Rational Self-Counseling sessions, my patients listen daily to our professionally recorded nondrinking lecture, followed by a self-recorded nondrinking script.*

---

*Chapter 13 gives you a detailed description of those tapes and how I use them.

My research indicates that when patients are confused about simple facts, they usually resolve their confusion fastest by merely listening to those facts on tape. That's why I was content to switch back to a topic Bob already understood: cigarette addiction. My main therapeutic goal for this session was to get him to see that de-addiction was just a matter of rational mind over irrational gut.

Dr. M.: Actually, in one way it made more sense for you to get addicted to alcohol than to cigarettes.
Bob: Oh! Why is that?
Dr. M.: Because if you didn't drink too much too fast the first few times you drank, your first few experiences with alcohol were probably pleasant, especially if you were drinking mixed drinks. Right?
Bob: Yeah, I really liked the taste and everything right from the start.
Dr. M.: But I bet that wasn't the case with your first cigarette. Your first cigarette was probably a miserable experience. I know mine was. I threw up, got a headache, had a bad taste in my mouth; I really got sick! You would think that after

an otherwise healthy, intelligent kid had gotten over such a miserable experience, he would say "Cigarettes are not for me," and never smoke another one. And many kids do. But not me; Oh no! Just as soon as I had recovered enough from that first one, I smoked another one and another one, and on and on until I made myself a cigarette addict. Now, why do you think I did that?

Bob: (Smiling) I guess because you wanted to.

Dr. M.: Right, but why did I want to? It was because I wanted to be like the tough guys in the movies; and I thought that if I smoked like they did, I would be more of the "he-man" I irrationally believed they were. So I refused to be satisfied with the self-image of me being such a kid, that I couldn't smoke my cigarettes as good as any man. (laughter)

Bob: Did you try drinking, too?

Dr. M.: Not until I got to college. Where I grew up they really didn't allow kids to buy alcohol. And my parents didn't allow it in the house, so I was never directly exposed to it. My parents didn't smoke either. But almost everybody else did; and we kids could hide smoking from our parents pretty easily. But the point is I diligently worked at learning how to smoke, even though at first my body violently resisted. That's why I keep reminding you of what a powerful organ your brain is and that it's how you program it with your thoughts that decides the type of self-control you have. In my case, my irrational beliefs about myself as a nonsmoking kid programmed my brain to make me mentally dependent on cigarettes for a positive self-image, even before I had smoked my first one. And my irrational hope to get rid of that negative self-image by smoking was all I needed to keep me putting myself through the miserable experience of learning to smoke. But I controlled the whole thing. I created my own negative self-image as well as my positive thoughts about smoking; and I alone maintained and acted on them over and over again. That's my point. You follow me?

Bob: I think so; but you see my problem is different. I mean, many times I've thought about how bad drinking is for me;

	and a few times I have honestly decided that I never wanted to see another drink. But, I always keep on feeling like I really do want one; so I end up thinking, "What am I trying to fool myself for? Deep down I must really want that drink." So, I always ended up taking it and all the others I get my hands on.

Dr. M.: I understand that. It's a common, confusing experience, not only for people who want to stop drinking but also for people who want to stop smoking. That's why I use the cigarette example to show problem drinkers how to clear up that confusion. And once they stop being confused, that frees them to stop doing what they really don't want to do in the first place. Tell me, how much do you smoke a day?

Bob: About a pack and a half a day.

Dr. M.: Okay, that means every forty-five minutes to an hour when you are awake you normally have a cigarette in your mouth, right?

Bob: Right!

Dr. M.: Before you light up, do you first think, "I want a cigarette, therefore, I will smoke one right now?"

Bob: Not usually. I just sort of smoke without thinking much about it, unless I don't have any.

Dr. M.: Right! That's because your body is so dependent on tobacco now that every forty-five minutes or so you automatically get an inner urge or primary craving for a smoke. Right?

Bob: Right!

Dr. M.: And if you are out of cigarettes, you start thinking "I need a cigarette, I've got to have a cigarette." And those thoughts cause you to start looking for a cigarette. And you probably don't stop looking or thinking those thoughts until you find yourself a smoke. Right?

Bob: (Smiling) Right! I have even rolled up newspaper and smoked it in the middle of the night when I ran out of cigarettes. But I don't do that any more. They don't make newspapers the way they used to. The last time I tried it, I got sick as a dog. I guess they make it taste so bad to discourage the kids from doing it.

SELF DISCLOSURE IN RSC

Normally in Rational Self-Counseling Sessions counselors keep the discussion focused on the patient. But if counselors have potentially helpful past experiences, **they can freely share them, provided:**

1. The experience is both over and was successfully handled.

AND

2. The patient can readily identify in a self-instructive way with the counselor in that past situation.

Otherwise, I advise against self disclosures by counselors. I see no value in having patients pay to listen to the unresolved, irrelevant experiences of their counselors.

Next, I will share with Bob my experience in de-addicting myself to cigarettes. Notice how readily he identifies with it in a self-instructive way.

THE PROCESS OF DE-ADDICTION

Dr. M.: Okay, so we can safely say you're a real cigarette addict. Now let's talk about the process of de-addiction. When I was a medical student, I was smoking two packs of cigarettes per day, pretty much like you do now. But I had a part-time job helping do autopsies; and after three or four on people who had died from lung cancer, I decided, "Hey, smoking is really bad for my health. Since I really want to die of old age, I had better stop smoking right away." That belief made my situation with my problem smoking similar to yours with problem drinking.

Bob: So what did you do?

Dr. M.: I handled it rationally. By that I mean I looked at the objective reality: that to get rid of any drug habit, you first have to create and maintain a sincere desire to get rid of it. To do that you have to perceive the unwanted habit at A; and at B, you must continuously have ideas of WANTING to get rid of that habit. Now, even after I sincerely took that first step, about a half hour after my last cigarette, how do you think I felt?

Bob: You wanted a cigarette.

Dr. M.: No, not really; but that's the common mistake addicts make. I DIDN'T want a cigarette, I just FELT as if I wanted one. But I knew for a fact that I neither wanted, nor desired, nor needed one. In reality, I desired not to smoke and I proved it by refusing to smoke. That's the key insight to make here—the important difference between wanting a smoke or a drink versus craving, or feeling as if you want a smoke or drink, when in fact you really don't want to smoke or drink. If problem drinkers don't make that distinction, they get confused and end up jumping off the wagon.

Bob: But how can you stay out of that trap?

Dr. M.: The same way I did. After I decided not to smoke any more, I refused to give in to my craving for a smoke. And by refusing to give in, I both maintained and reinforced my desire not to smoke. But to do that I had to keep my

	thinking straight because thinking really controls everything else.
Bob:	I see what you mean; but my cravings are so overpowering they just take over.
Dr. M.:	No, no, no! They don't take over; you just give in. And it's lucky for you that's all there is to it. If your cravings really were overpowering, you could never solve your problem. But if you keep your thinking straight, you can solve it quite easily.
Bob:	Okay, what is the secret?
Dr. M.:	It's no secret. All you have to do is remember and act on this fact: There are two kinds of cravings, primary and secondary. The primary cravings are the ones you can't prevent, but you still don't have to give in to them. If you make up your mind, you can wait them out. Now with cigarette addiction that's okay; but with advanced alcoholism I recommend that you get medical care to get over your primary alcoholic craving; otherwise you might die. But once all the drug is out of your body, and your body readjusts itself to life without the drug, your primary cravings automatically stop for good.
Bob:	Yeah, but it takes so long.
Dr. M.:	Not really. Usually it's no more than two or three days.
Bob:	Mine lasts much longer than that. Even after nine months in jail, I couldn't make it past the first bar.
Dr. M.:	It wasn't that you couldn't, it's just that you didn't. And those were not primary cravings; they were secondary cravings. They are the ones you had been practicing for nine months in prison. That's why you were so good at having them.
Bob:	(puzzled) Practicing? How do you mean practicing? I didn't even see a drink while I was locked up.

YOU LEARN ONLY IN YOUR BRAIN

To get patients to see clearly how they can practice mentally without performing physical actions, I tell them about Pavlov and how he taught his dogs to salivate to the sound of a bell. Then I tell them about a psychologist who used to begin class by telling his students to close their eyes and visualize a thick, juicy T-bone steak with onions and all the trimmings. Because the class met at 11:00 a.m. the students could easily put themselves completely into the experiment. When the students began to visualize the steak, the professor would start a metronome ticking.

After a few minutes, the professor would turn off the metronome and begin his lecture.

Every day for a few weeks the professor started his class with that routine. Then one day the professor skipped that routine and started his lecture and metronome immediately. A few minutes later he asked the students if they noticed anything unusual. Several of them noticed that they were copiously salivating.

After I told Bob about that experiment, it was easy to get him to see clearly how he had maintained his craving for alcohol even though he was in jail and couldn't get it.

Dr. M.: Do you remember what you told me last week about how you passed your time in jail?

Bob: (Smiling) You're talking about how I used to daydream about all the partying I was going to do to celebrate getting out?

Dr. M.: Right. You did the same thing with your thoughts of alcohol and celebrating that those students did with their thoughts of steaks and the metronome. Without realizing it you both mentally practiced reacting on cue, the students on cue of the metronome and you on cue of the first bar you passed. But the key insight is: just as you used **your** brain to keep your alcoholic cravings going strong, had you known how, you could have used your brain to eliminate them. And if you had done that, you would have stayed sober on your first day out of prison, and as many other days as you wanted to.

Bob: But how could I handle the craving?

Dr. M.: The same way I handled my craving for cigarettes. At first, after I had smoked my last cigarette, every forty-five

Bob: minutes or so I felt as if I wanted to smoke; but I just kept telling myself: "I don't want to smoke; I actually want not to smoke." Then to prove it, I refused to smoke. And pretty soon, what do you think happened to my cravings?
Bob: They left?
Dr. M.: Exactly! Of course a half-hour or so later for two or three days they came back; but I kept on calmly ignoring them just one more time than they came back. And as soon as all the nicotine and other chemicals were out of my body, I was almost home free. I say "almost" because I still had to get myself out of the stage of mental dependence on cigarettes with all its external cues for smoking to enjoy myself. But my "just-one-more-time" routine made that relatively easy.
Bob: How did it work?
Dr. M.: Simple. I just refused to give in to my craving, one more time than I got it. BUT! even though I only had to do it one more time, **I had to do it every time.**
Bob: But I can't believe you can handle a drinking problem that easy.
Dr. M.: Well, alcohol does present a little bit of a different problem: It really does temporarily make you feel less miserable emotionally. Cigarettes usually don't have much effect on your emotions. So, in that sense, getting rid of an alcohol habit may require a bit more rational mental effort than getting rid of a cigarette habit.
Bob: Yeah, I think so.
Dr. M.: But, the facts about stopping smoking apply equally well to stopping drinking. That's the main point I want you to remember. The first step is always a sincere decision to stop. The next step is to change your thinking about drinking and, and—that's a big "and"—you have to keep your thinking changed. You have never done that before. Like most problem drinkers, all you have done is get dried out, and out of the stage of physical dependence. But you have always kept yourself in advanced stage one by continuing to believe alcohol is the only way you can cope with your problems and enjoy life. And that belief has kept your

	secondary alcoholic cravings strong. That's why you have always ended up jumping off the wagon. Right?
Bob:	Yeah, that's about it.
Dr. M.:	Well, the fastest first step that I know of for getting out of stage one of problem drinking is systematic written Rational Self-Analysis. And that's what I want you to read about in this little booklet entitled "The ABC's of Rational Self-Analysis." Read it once a day every day until I see you next week; and after the second reading, try to do an RSA of a past event that usually ended with you getting drunk. I'll go over it with you to see what kind of changes in your thinking you will have to make to keep yourself from getting drunk in that situation again. Okay?

EMPHASIS QUESTIONS

1. After I (Dr. Maultsby) sincerely decided to stop smoking, I never ever had the urge to smoke again. True or False?
2. Forty minutes or so after my last cigarette I really didn't want to smoke another one, even though I felt as if I really did want to smoke again. True or False?
3. If you feel as if you need something, you must really need it, even though you think you don't. True or False?
4. When problem drinkers don't distinguish between _____ a drink and _____ as if they _____ a drink, they often get confused and end up _____ off the _____.
5. Bob's secondary alcoholic cravings were so overpowering they just took over control of him. True or False?
6. There are _____ kinds of craves: _____ and _____.
7. Addicts can't _____ their _____ craves.
8. To maintain secondary craves, you have to _____ them.
9. RSA is short for _____ _____ _____.
10. One of the fastest ways for people to get themselves over their obsessive stage of problem drinking is doing systematic, written _____ _____ _____.
11. To force your body to stop depending on alcohol or cigarettes, you must _____ to drink or smoke and let your body get

completely _____ of the alcohol or the tobacco chemicals.
12. To stop secondary alcohol craving fast, you must _____ to _____ in to it.
13. Rational Self-Counseling helps you feel better _____ alcoholic drinking.
14. To stop problem drinking, people must make a sincere _____ to stop drinking; then they must change their _____ about _____ and keep their _____ changed.

CORRECT ANSWERS

1. False
2. True
3. False
4. wanting, feeling, want, jumping, wagon
5. False
6. two, primary, secondary
7. prevent, primary
8. practice
9. Rational Self-Analysis
10. Rational Self-Analysis
11. refuse, free
12. refuse, give
13. without
14. decision, thinking, drinking, thinking

SECTION II

(Part Two)

The following chapters give you detailed descriptions of the main self-help techniques used for Rational Self-Counseling. They are the same self-help techniques routinely used by Rational Behavior and Rational Emotive Therapists. (Professional Acknowledgement page.)

Chapter 10 The ABC's of Rational Self-Analysis
Chapter 11 Rational Emotive Imagery
Chapter 12 Using RSA's For Treatment
Chapter 13 Why Your Attitude Is The "IT" that Upsets You
Chapter 14 From Drinking To Non-drinking Behavior

Most problem drinkers particularly like chapter 14. It gives them straightforward detailed information about the five stages in behavioral re-education problem drinkers must master to solve their drinking problem. In addition chapter 14 describes the rational practice technique for eliminating the compulsive urge to drink.

10

The ABC's of Rational Self-Analysis

Rational Self-Analysis (RSA) is a quick, easy way to analyze, solve, and prevent personal problems. It is also a quick, easy way to analyze your personal successes to see how to keep them happening.

HOW TO DO AN RSA

Write up a personal event:

—Immediately (if possible)
—In your everyday language, and
—In the standard RSA Format

THE STANDARD RSA FORMAT

A. Activating Events

B. Beliefs
    B-1
    B-2
    etc.

C. Consequences of B
    I. Emotional Feelings
    II. Physical Actions

Da. Camera Check of A

Db. Rational Debate of B
    Db-1
    Db-2
    etc.

E. Expected New Behaviors
    I. New Emotions
    II. New Physical Actions

THE FIVE QUESTIONS FOR RATIONAL THINKING

1. Is my thinking here factual?
2. Will my thinking here help me protect myself from probable harm?
3. Will my thinking here help me achieve my short-term and long-term goals?
4. Will my thinking here help me avoid significant conflict with others?
5. Will my thinking here help me habitually feel the emotions I want to feel?

FIRST

On the left half of your paper, write A, the activating event. Simply state the relevant facts as you saw and experienced them. Relevant facts are the important ones to remember in similar future situations. In her first RSA Mrs. Green wrote about these facts:

A. Activating Event Da. Camera Check of A
Chuck started picking on
me about drinking. It
made me so mad I had to
take a drink to calm down.

The camera check often takes up to four times as many lines as the activating event. That's why Mrs. Green left twelve lines blank between her A section and her B section.

SECOND

Write B, your beliefs. Record your actual self-talk during and after the A section event. Number each B section idea; and immediately after you write it, decide which of the following three attitudes you have about it: good, bad, or neutral. Write that word in parentheses after the statement. Mrs. Green's B section was:

B. Beliefs	Db. Rational Debate of B
B-1 He's always picking on me just because I take a little drink now and then—the CREEP! (bad)	Db-1

It usually takes about six times as many lines to analyze a B-section idea as it takes to write it. That's why Mrs. Green left eighteen blank lines between her B-1 and her B-2 ideas.

After you complete the B section, count up your goods, bads, and neutrals. Your count will show you the main type of attitudes that caused your brain to trigger the emotional feelings and actions you had about A, the activating event.

THIRD

Write C, the consequences of B. The C section has two parts: Emotional Feelings and Physical Actions. In the appropriate part write simple statements of fact about how you felt, and what you did. For example, Mrs. Green wrote:

C. The Consequences of B	E. Expected New Behaviors
I. Emotional Feelings	I. New Emotions
1. Angry at Chuck	1.
2. Felt like I needed a drink	2.
II. Physical Action	II. New Physical Actions
1. Kept on drinking	1.

FOURTH

Write the five questions for Rational Thinking under the C section.
1. Is my thinking here factual?
2. Will my thinking here help me protect myself from probable harm?

3. Will my thinking here help me achieve my short-term and long-term goals?
4. Will my thinking here help me avoid significant conflict with others?
5. Will my thinking here help me habitually feel the emotions I want to feel?

FIFTH

Write Da, camera check of A. The camera check helps you get the most benefit from your brain's camera-like functions. First, you ask, then honestly answer this question: Would a movie camera have recorded the facts as I did? If your answer is "Yes" for each A-section sentence, simply write "Factual" or "All Facts" in the Da section and go on to the B section. But if you have a "No" answer, that shows you substituted your opinion for a factual statement. Correct that statement to what a movie camera would have recorded. For example, parents who are angry about their son's failure to clean his room would correct the opinion: "My son is as lazy as the devil" to "My son doesn't clean his room unless I tell him to."

Yes, they have a right to their opinions; but opinions are beliefs; they belong in the Belief Section. (See below Mrs. Green's camera check of A.)

A.	Activating Event Chuck started picking on me about drinking. It made me so mad I had to take a drink to calm down.	Da.	Camera Check of A Chuck didn't pick on me. He didn't even touch me. I didn't let him get that close to me. I was afraid he'd smell the gin on my breath. It didn't make me angry. I didn't have to take that drink. I chose to drink it.

No, I don't believe that cameras always record the obvious facts; but if a camera could not have recorded an A-section description, that description will probably be more opinion than fact. To learn the most emotionally healthy self-control, however, people must learn to keep their opinions and facts separated.

A camera cannot record emotional feelings. But emotional feelings are psycho-physiologic facts. You either feel them or you don't; you either describe them accurately or you don't; and you are the only one who can do either. That's why you can put simple statements of emotional fact, such as, "I was sad" or "I felt depressed," in your A section. But you would still rewrite them in the emotional feelings part of your C section.

When your A section is an emotional feeling, simply write FACTUAL for your camera check of A. But if you describe an embarrassment with, "I felt I was dying," correct it to: "I didn't feel as if I were really dying; but I felt so embarrassed, I wanted to leave."

SIXTH

Write your Db section. That's where you rationally debate your B section beliefs. First, read over your B-1 statement. Then answer this question, "Can I give three or more honest "Yes" answers when I check that idea with the Five Questions For Rational Thinking? If you can, merely write: "That's rational" at Db-1. If you cannot come up with at least three honest "Yes's," think of a different way of thinking about that situation; but make sure that your new way of thinking has these two features:

1. The new ideas deserve at least three honest "Yes's" from you for the Five Questions For Rational Thinking.

AND

2. You are willing to make those new ideas your personal beliefs about that and similar future A-type situations.

Remember, it doesn't matter how rational an idea may be: if you are not willing to make it your personal belief and act on it, it won't help you.

B.	Beliefs	Db.	Rational Debate of B
B-1	He's always picking on me just because I take a little drink now and then—the CREEP! (bad)	Db-1	My answer to RQ #1* is NO; to RQ #2 is DNA**; to RQ #3 is NO; to RQ #4 is NO; to RQ #5 is NO. I had 0 "yes" answers; therefore, my thinking here is IRRATIONAL. Rational thinking for me would have been: He never picks on me, even when I get sloppy drunk. He's not a creep. He's just a FHB*** who's trying to get along better with a wife who drinks too much. And I'm going to start helping him do it today by RATIONALLY refusing to drink so much; or even better, not to drink at all.

---

*RQ means rational question.
**DNA means Does Not Apply.
***FHB is short for Fallible Human Being, rational substitute for SOB.

Some of your B section ideas will be questions. A common one is the angrily asked "How could they do such a thing?" (bad). But you cannot rationally debate questions; you can debate only the rationality of your answers to questions.

For the angrily asked "How could they do such a thing?" (bad), most really rational thinkers would write: "EASILY! By just acting out the idea of doing it." That statement of probable fact, plus (bad) written after the question, lets people quickly separate the facts—somebody took an action—from their personal opinions or attitudes that it was bad for them that the action was taken; and that who ever took it shouldn't have done it.

If people do something, their action is a fact. But a fact can't be rational or irrational; only beliefs about facts have those two options. That's why only the people who take an action can really decide if it was a rational action to have taken. Ideally, they will make that decision rationally. But you will be working on YOUR RSA, not on theirs. That's why you are to debate only the rationality of your attitudes that the action taken was bad for you, and that the people who took it shouldn't have taken it.

SEVENTH

Write E, Expected New Behaviors. That's where you describe the new emotional and physical reactions you want to learn to have in future A-type situations. These reactions are not to be "Oh, if I only had . . ." type wishes. Instead, they are to be your personally chosen emotional and **physical goals for your future.**

C. Consequences of B
    I. Emotional Feelings
        1. angry at Chuck
        2. felt like I needed a drink

    II. Physical Action
        1. kept on drinking

E. Expected New Behaviors
    I. New Emotions
        1. calm when Chuck mentions alcohol
        2. not to feel like I need a drink to feel better

    II. New Physical Action
        1. refuse to get drunk any more.

Remember, your E-section goals must be logical for your Db-section. It's a waste of time to write "To feel calm" under E if among your Db beliefs you have written: "It really is awful"; "I really can't stand it; I know I'll just die if they do it again."*

And they won't, because they can't. So don't worry about it. RSA's cannot and therefore will not stop people from having emotions.

Don't be so naive as to believe that if you stop feeling more emotional pain than you want to, you will stop feeling altogether. That just can't happen to physically healthy people.

The minds of physically healthy people force their brains to trigger and maintain some type of emotional state every second they are awake. So, if you are healthy, undrugged, and conscious, you will always have some type of an emotion. It may not be the one you want but you will definitely have one. Consequently, an E section

---

*Some people prefer to write the E section immediately after the C section. That too is all right. But don't forget to write the five questions for rational thinking afterwards.

that reads "I want to have no feelings at all" is meaningless. You can't achieve that emotional goal and remain conscious and healthy.

The only two things RSA can do are:

1. help you have more of the emotions you like to have without alcohol or other drugs, and

2. help you have fewer of the emotions you don't like to have.

MRS. GREEN'S COMPLETE RSA

A. Activating Event
Chuck started picking on me about drinking. It made me so mad I had to take a drink to calm down.

Da. Camera Check of A
Chuck didn't pick on me. He didn't even touch me. I didn't let him get that close to me. I was afraid he'd smell the gin on my breath. It didn't make me angry. I made me angry. I didn't have to take that drink. I chose to drink it.

B. Beliefs

B-1 He's always picking on me just because I take a little drink now and then—the CREEP! (bad)

Db. Rational Debate of B

Db-1 My answer to RQ #1 is NO; to RQ #2 is DNA; to RQ #3 is NO; to RQ #4 is NO; to RQ #5 is NO. I had 0 "yes" answers; therefore, my thinking here is IRRATIONAL. Rational thinking for me would have been: He never picks on me, even when I get sloppy drunk. He's not a creep. He's just a FHB who's trying to get along better with a wife who drinks too much. And I'm going to start helping him do it today by

		RATIONALLY refusing to drink so much; or even better, not to drink at all.
B-2	He always accuses me of being drunk. (bad)	Db-2	My answer to RQ #1 is NO; to RQ #2 is DNA; to RQ #3 is NO; to RQ #4 is NO; to RQ #5 is NO. I had 0 "yes" answers; therefore, my thinking here is IR-RATIONAL. Rational thinking for me would have been: He rarely accuses me of being drunk, even when I really am drunk. I made myself irrationally angry about nothing. And I'm going to get rid of that habit as soon as possible, starting today.
B-3	He's lying. He doesn't believe me. (bad)	Db-3	My answer to RQ #1 is NO; to RQ #2 is DNA; to RQ #3 is NO; to RQ #4 is NO; to RQ #5 is NO. I have 0 "yes" answers; therefore, my thinking here is IR-RATIONAL. Rational thinking for me would have been: I have no rational reason to believe he's lying; so I'll stop believing it now.
B-4	He thinks I drank it all. It wasn't that much anyway. (bad)	Db-4	My answer to RQ #1 is NO; to RQ #2 is DNA; to RQ #3 is NO; to RQ #4 is NO; to RQ #5 is NO. I had 0 "yes" answers; therefore

my thinking is IRRATIONAL. Rational thinking for me would have been I don't know what he thinks, but if he thinks I drank it all he's half right. But now I'm going to prove him to be half wrong by refusing to drink the other half.

B-5 Since he doesn't believe me anyway, I may as well make it true and enjoy myself. (bad)

Db-5 My answer to RQ #1 is NO; to RQ #2 is DNA; to RQ #3 is NO; to RQ #4 is NO; to RQ #5 is NO. I had 0 "yes" answers; therefore, my thinking here is IRRATIONAL. Rational thinking would have been: I don't know whether he believes me or not; and it really doesn't matter. But if I drink any more today, I'll be the one with the hangover tomorrow. So I refuse to take another drink. I can think myself to a better feeling without it.

B-6 I need a refill. To hell with him! (bad)

Db-6 My answer to RQ #1 is NO; to RQ #2 is DNA; to RQ #3 is NO; to RQ #4 is NO; to RQ #5 is NO. I had 0 "yes" answers; therefore, my thinking here is IRRATIONAL. Rational thinking would have been:

"I don't need another drink; and I refuse to take one."

When Mrs. Green counted up her bad's she thought: "No wonder I felt so bad; all my attitudes were very bad."

C.   Consequence of B
    I. Emotional Feelings
      (1) angry at Chuck
      (2) felt like I needed a drink

    II. Physical Action
      (1) kept on drinking

E.   Expected New Behaviors
    I. New Emotions
      (1) calm when Chuck mentions alcohol
      (2) not to feel like I need a drink to feel better

    II. New Physical Action
      (1) refuse to get drunk any more

THE FIVE QUESTIONS FOR RATIONAL THINKING

1. Is my thinking here factual?
2. Will my thinking here help me to protect myself from probable harm?
3. Will my thinking help me efficiently achieve my short-term and long-term goals?
4. Will my thinking help me avoid significant conflict with others?
5. Will my thinking help me habitually feel the emotions I want to feel?

A WELL DONE RSA

That's the FIRST STEP toward the most emotionally healthy self-control. But neither one nor even fifty well done RSA's will solve your problems. Your well-done RSA's only give you the mental maps for solving your problems. But maps can't help you unless you follow them. That's another way of saying: To reach your emotional and other personal goals, you must put your RSA's into practice, ideally daily practice.

"No, but at first most people get the most help the fastest by writing their RSA's as soon as possible after a personally undesirable event. Many people, however, skip the writing and try to do RSA's in their heads. But all they usually get is confused. Short-cuts on RSA's are silly games people play with themselves that have no winners— and only they can lose."*

A WELL DONE RSA PER DAY HELPS KEEP ALCOHOL ABUSE AWAY

EMPHASIS QUESTIONS

1. RSA is a quick, easy way to analyze and solve personal problems. True or False?
2. When doing an RSA, it's best not to take _____ cuts.

---

*This chapter is available as a booklet: "The ABC's of Rational Self-Analysis" for $1.50 from The RBT Center, College of Medicine, University of Kentucky, Lexington, Ky., 40506. Bulk prices available.

3. Short-cuts on your RSA's are _____ games with _____ that usually have _____ winner and only you can _____.

4. Written _____ help you stay in the most _____ healthy _____ control.

5. It's best to write your RSA's down. True or False?

6. Well done RSA's of happy events show you how lucky you are. True or False?

7. To do an RSA correctly, you follow the _____ format.

8. In an RSA you first write how you want to learn to behave. True or False?

9. After each B statement, you put your _____ about it in parentheses.

10. In writing an RSA first you write the _____, then _____, then _____ sections on the _____ side of your paper.

11. After you write the B section of your RSA, you write the _____ and the _____ questions for _____ thinking, then _____ check of _____ and then Db or _____ of B.

12. If a movie camera could not have recorded your description of an event, the description was probably subjective opinion. True or False?

13. The camera _____ applies only to _____ events, and not to emotions.

14. RSA's deny you your right to have personal opinions. True or False?

15. An honest "NO" answer to any one of the five rational questions proves that the idea being debated is irrational. True or False?

16. It takes at least three honest "YES" answers to demonstrate that the idea being debated is rational. True or False?

17. Improved emotional self-control _____ you to have _____ of the _____ you _____ to _____.

18. Written Rational Self-_____ is an _____ self-help technique routinely taught to people receiving Rational Behavior Therapy, or who are learning Rational Self-Counseling.

19. A well done RSA does not solve your problems. True or False?

20. A well done RSA is the _____ step toward solving your _____ rationally.

CORRECT ANSWERS

1. True
2. short
3. silly, yourself, no, lose
4. RSA's, emotionally, self
5. True
6. False
7. standard
8. False
9. attitude
10. A, B, C, left
11. C section, five, rational, camera, A, rational debate
12. True
13. check, external
14. False
15. False
16. True
17. enables, more, emotions, want or like, have
18. analysis, emotional
19. True
20. first, problem

11

Rational Emotive Imagery

Most emotionally distressed people want to improve their emotional control, but they usually don't believe they can do it. So they make excuses such as: "Yes, I know I'd be better off if I controlled my emotions better. And I've tried. Really!! But I just can't do it. My emotions just take over. That's just me, a bundle of emotions."

Fortunately those people are wrong. Undesirable emotional habits are not people; **they are just undesirable habits.** When people practice the improved thinking needed to improve their emotional control, they improve it. Unfortunately, most people never learn to associate practice with learning new emotional habits. That's why they don't practice. Instead, they either wait for a miraculous emotional rebirth or they try to trick themselves into feeling better without doing the needed practice in thinking better. In both cases, therefore, they end up maintaining their undesirable emotional habits and the incorrect belief that they can't change.

Improved emotional control requires practice. **All practice takes place in the brain.** The following experiment in improved self-control demonstrates that psychosomatic fact quite clearly.

A psychologist gathered together three groups of women of similar age and health who had never played basketball. He paid them the same amount for trying to shoot fifty free throws. How many they missed was irrelevant. There was no significant difference between the group totals of missed free throws.

After the test, group one was paid to sit fifteen minutes every day for a week and think about shooting free throws.

Group two was paid to practice shooting free throws for fifteen minutes every day for that week. Group three was paid (the same amount as groups one and two) just to return for a retest one week later.

At the retest groups one and two missed significantly fewer free throws than group three. But group two missed only slightly fewer free throws than group one. In addition, the better free throw shooter in group one missed significantly fewer free throws than the worst free throw shooter in group two.

Those results reveal two important facts:

1. There are two kinds of practice:
   a. mental-emotive practice (Group one)
   b. mental-emotive-physical practice (Group two)
2. Mental-emotive practice produces the same type of learning as mental-emotive-physical practice produces.

My clinical research and that of many others shows that emotional learning follows the same principles of practice that free throw shooting follows.

Rational Emotive Imagery (REI) is an intense form of mental-emotive practice for learning new emotional habits. When people combine REI with mental-emotive-physical practice, they learn new emotional as well as physical habits in the shortest possible time. That's why Rational Emotive Imagery is the second most important self-help technique in Rational Self-Counseling.

HASTE USUALLY MAKES THE LEAST SPEED

I remind people of that fact when they get the urge to skip writing their RSA's and immediately start doing REI. The rational rule is: always do a Rational Self-Analysis before Rational Emotive Imagery. Otherwise you may unwittingly end up practicing your old habits, failing to improve, and incorrectly accusing REI of not working.

For the fastest and safest results with REI follow these steps:
(1) First read the Da, Db, and E sections of the RSA you will practice with REI.
(2) Get relaxed.

THE INSTANT CALMING MANEUVER (ICM)

For quick, easy relaxation, first get physically comfortable while standing, sitting, or preferably lying down. Next, close your eyes and slow your breathing rate to between four and six complete intake-output cycles per minute.

Begin by gently taking in a somewhat deeper than normal

breath without significantly exerting yourself; then without holding your breath, gently but firmly breathe that air out completely; hold your breath, and mentally count a thousand-one, a thousand-two, and on up to a thousand-ten, if that's comfortable for you. Then repeat the above breathing cycle. The main idea is to do slow, comfortable, relaxed breathing. So stop counting and breathe in at a thousand-six or seven if that's most comfortable for you.

In the beginning, time yourself with a second hand. The most calming intake-output cycles take four to five seconds. By holding your breath from six to ten seconds (it takes about a second to think a thousand-and-one) you will be breathing between four and six times per minute. It's almost impossible not to relax if you keep breathing at that slow rate.

Continue the ICM for three minutes or until you are noticeably relaxed. Then go to step three.

(3) While keeping your eyes closed, picture yourself as vividly as possible back in your Da situation.

(4) Maintain that image while thinking your rational Db thoughts. If B section thoughts pop into your mind, calmly challenge them with your Db thoughts.

(5) As you vividly picture yourself being in the Da situation, thinking and saying your rational Db thoughts, imagine yourself having your E section emotional feelings and physical behavior. Make the experience as realistic and vivid as possible.

(6) Repeat that imagery over and over for ten minutes. If you have two RSA's for practice, spend five minutes on each. But don't do REI on more than two RSA's during one ten-minute REI session.

OLD HABITS DON'T DISAPPEAR JUST BECAUSE YOU DON'T WANT THEM ANYMORE

So, don't expect an emotional miracle after just one REI session. Instead do REI on the same habit for ten minutes every day until you get the results you want. REMEMBER, to get rid of old habits you have to replace them. That takes time and repeated practice.

DAILY RECOMMENDED REI ROUTINE

(1) Put yourself to sleep with REI. It's cheaper, safer, and quicker than sleeping pills.
(2) Ten minutes just before you get out of bed each morning. Morning REI's let you start your day with pleasantly powerful emotional feelings associated with confidence of success.

(3) Ten minutes just before lunch or instead of cigarette breaks. Then you will be fighting lung cancer, heart disease and bad breath at the same time.
(4) Ten minutes before your first afternoon cocktail. That way you are more likely to remember eating and enjoying your dinner.

You can also do REI with your eyes open: while driving or riding to work, waiting in lines, waiting in traffic, or waiting for someone who's late. At those times REI will help keep your blood pressure down and prevent tension headaches.

By following that daily schedule you will be reprogramming your brain for your new, more rational behavior in the shortest time possible for you. Soon both you and your friends will begin to notice your positive changes.

REI ON RELATED EVENTS

After you have practiced your RSA for four or five minutes, switch to related scenes that are logical for your E section goals.

That type of daily comprehensive emotional practice enabled Mrs. Green to improve her emotional control before she returned home. That's why she succeeded this time, even though she had failed several times before.

WELL-DONE REI EVERY DAY REALLY DOES KEEP ALCOHOL ABUSE AWAY

EMPHASIS QUESTIONS

1. REI is an intense form of _____-emotive _____.
2. Physically healthy people do _____ practice without realizing it.
3. Undesirable emotional habits are usually just _____.
4. There are two kinds of practice:
   (a) mental-_____ practice
   (b) mental-_____-_____ practice.
5. Haste usually makes the _____ speed.
6. The rational rule is always do a _____ _____-_____ before doing REI.
7. The main idea of the ICM is to do slow, comfortable, relaxed _____.
8. It's best to practice no more than two RSA's in any one ten-minute REI sessions. True or False?
9. Do REI on your new _____ for at least ten minutes every day.
10. Instead of doing emotional _____, most people wait for _____ emotional _____.
11. If people know how to do _____, they won't have to wait until a real situation occurs to _____ better self-control.
12. That's because (item #1) all _____ takes place in the _____ of the learner.
13. Old habits _____ disappear just because you don't _____ them anymore.
14. You can't do REI with your eyes open. True or False?
15. To get rid of old habits you have to replace them with new ones. True or False?

CORRECT ANSWERS

1. mental, practice
2. emotional
3. habits
4. emotive, emotive-physical
5. least
6. Rational Self-Analysis
7. breathing
8. True
9. emotions
10. practice, miraculous, rebirths
11. REI, practice
12. learning, brain
13. don't, want
14. False
15. True

PLEASE NOTE

This chapter is available as a booklet: "What Your Rational Mind Conceives, You Can Achieve", for $1.50 from The RBT Center, College of Medicine, University of Kentucky, Lexington, Ky., 40506. Bulk prices available.

12

Using RSA's for Treatment

A well done RSA a day helps keep alcohol abuse away. That's why I encourage patients to do an RSA any time they are more upset than they want to be. It doesn't matter how trivial a problem may seem; if it was worth getting upset about, it's worth a rational analysis. In fact, well-done RSA's quickly show that most seemingly overwhelming problems in daily living are just exaggerations of objectively trivial events. But I rarely tell patients that; they benefit most when they discover it for themselves. And they make that discovery most quickly if they use this rational rule of thumb: **No undesirable thought, feeling, or action is too trivial to be analyzed rationally.**

HOW TO DO THERAPY WITH RSA'S*

Diligent patients usually bring more than one RSA to their treatment sessions, but we rarely cover more than one. Conse-

---

*RSA sessions can be as short as fifteen minutes or as long as two hours. I recommend that one to two hour sessions be restricted to small groups of four to ten patients.

quently, I have patients choose the most important RSA (to them) and I structure the session around it.

If the hour runs out before we finish I simply ask patients to put a check mark at the stopping point. At the next session we start there, unless the patient then has a more important RSA.

A well done RSA usually produces several helpful insights. But patients rarely will put into daily practice more than one or two new insights per week. That's why no harm is done if the session ends before the RSA. In addition, the more thoroughly patients discuss their rational insights, the more likely they are to act them out.

If we complete an RSA before the session is over, I do one of two things: I use the remaining time to discuss how to apply the new-found insights to different life events; or I ask patients to start presenting their next most important RSA.

THE RSA SEQUENCE IN THERAPY

When patients write RSA's, they are to write them in this order: first A, then B, then C, then E, then the five questions for rational thinking, and finally Da and Db. In their individual and group sessions, however, I have patients present their RSA's in this order: first the A section, then the C section, then the E section. That gives me an immediate overview of the event, the patients' undesirable reaction to it, and how they want to learn to react in the future.

Next, I want to hear Da, the CAMERA CHECK of A. If I agree that a camera probably would have recorded the event as the patients described it, I reinforce them with: "That's good" or "Okay, I'll agree to that" or "That sounds factual to me, too."

If I disagree with patients' camera check of A, I tell them why; then we discuss the changes that would make the A section most factual. That discussion is straightforward and direct. For example, suppose a patient says: "A, I'm mad because she chewed me out in front of my staff." I'd say: "Show me the teeth marks." He'd say: "Come on, doc; you know what I mean." Then I'd say: "No, I don't know what you mean; I just know what you say. If she didn't chew, don't accuse her of it. Now tell me exactly what she did."

BOB'S FIRST RSA AS THERAPY*

Dr. M.: All right, let's hear your "A" section.

Bob: I moved into a quiet community of elderly people. My next door neighbor is a nosey old wench and the neighborhood's gossip-box. Twenty four hours a day she's prying into my personal affairs which don't concern her.

Dr. M.: Okay, now let's hear your C section.

Bob: Angry and upset.

---

*A video and audio tape of this session with explanations by Dr. Maultsby is available for professional training and educational use.

Write to Dr. Maxie C. Maultsby, Jr., Training Center For Rational Behavior Therapy and Emotional Self-Help, University of Kentucky Medical College, Lexington, Kentucky 40506.

Dr. M.: And what is your E section?
Bob: Calm. I want to feel calm with people like her.

With their first RSA's, patients often neither write nor use the Five Questions For Rational Thinking.

A COMMON MISTAKE TO AVOID

Inexperienced counselors sometimes accuse such patients of not really wanting to solve their problems. But in my experience that usually is not the real reason patients initially neglect the Five Questions For Rational Thinking. Most often such patients have just deceived themselves without realizing it.

UNWITTINGLY DECEIVING ONESELF
ABOUT RATIONAL THINKING

The Five Rules For Rational Thinking are obviously logical and sensible. When most people hear them, they quickly see that they have already been using those rules most of their lives. Unfortunately, though, such people don't usually realize that they still may not have been thinking rationally.

Often within a day, most people separately use all of the five rules for rational thinking. But for a thought to be rational, it must obey at least three of the five rules for rational thinking at the same time. Before learning to do RSA's, most people just assume that their thoughts are rational if they obey one or two of the five rules for rational thinking. Those people forget or ignore that irrational thoughts often obey one or two of those five rules, too. Consequently, before such people form the habit of making their thoughts obey at least three of the rational rules at the same time, they sometimes have irrational thoughts without realizing it.

To help patients quickly correct that mistake, after I hear their E section, I ask the new ones if they wrote the Five Questions For Rational Thinking. If they say they thought that step was unnecessary, I ask them to recite the five questions. If they can recite them, I have an appropriate reason to reinforce their knowing them. If patients cannot recite the questions, that gives me a logical reason to emphasize that the standard RSA format calls for writing those five questions immediately after the C section.

Writing the Five Questions For Rational Thinking requires patients to think of all of them. Furthermore, patients who write the questions are most likely to use all of them to debate their B-section ideas. When patients check their B-section ideas with all five of those questions, they quickly make a surprising discovery; their irrational ideas often obey one, and sometimes two of the Five Rules For Rational Thinking. Then patients begin to see why many of their old irrational beliefs had always seemed so rational to them.

After patients answer the Five Questions For Rational Thinking for a B-section idea, I have them label that idea as rational or irrational. That maneuver helps sensitize patients to the many irrational ideas that are commonly accepted as being rational.

I am quick to agree with rational sounding Db debates; and I'm equally quick to disagree with irrational sounding ones. When I disagree however, I always use the Five Questions For Rational Thinking in relation to their emotional and behavioral goals (described in their E section) to explain my disagreement.

Dr. M.: All right, did you write the five questions for rational thinking under your C section?

Bob: No, I just referred to them in the book.

Dr. M.: Well, in the future I suggest that you actually write them down. That's the quickest way to fix them in your mind. You may lose your book, but you will always have your mind with you. All right, let's hear your camera check of A.

Bob: It is a fact that the community is quiet and most of the people living there are old; but it's not a fact that my next door neighbor is a nosy old wench, or a twenty-four-hour-a-day gossip box. She's human, so she has to sleep sometime.

Dr. M.: Okay, that was a good factual correction of your subjective opinion about the lady. Now, tell me, can you notice any difference in the influence on your feelings between your first description of the lady and your second one?

Bob: Yes. In the first one I just sort of jumped to the first conclusion that I thought of.

Dr. M.: Okay, and what did you base that conclusion on?
Bob: How I felt.
Dr. M.: Exactly. That's the point I wanted you to see. At A you perceived your neighbor asking about your private affairs, and you immediately felt angry about it at C. And that led to angry thoughts about her.

Don't Get Confused There

It might seem as if I am implying that Bob's angry feelings caused his angry thoughts. That would be contradicting the A-B-C model of emotion (chapter 4). To avoid confusion, remember chapter 5 and the A-C or attitudinal form of habitual emotions.

Attitudes are the unspoken forms of habitual thoughts. The A-C model of habitual emotions indicates that Bob's angry attitude that his neighbor shouldn't be asking about his personal affairs triggered his anger. **But an emotion can't maintain itself; it has to be supported** with logical beliefs. So, to keep his anger from seeming to be illogical, Bob had to support it with sincere, angry thoughts. The first of his angry thoughts was his description of the lady. But his camera check clearly showed that he had not accurately described her.

Dr. M.: When you did the camera check what did you see?
Bob: My A section was plainly irrational thinking.
Dr. M.: Beautiful. You saw it's irrational to call a little old lady a twenty-four-hour-a-day gossip box when, in fact, she is just an F.H.B. who is doing something you don't want her to do. That's a very helpful insight. It shows you how important the camera check is for making sure you are focusing on objective facts, rather than on your irrational feelings or opinions about them.
Bob: I see what you mean.
Dr. M.: I want to emphasize that point because when people first start doing RSA's, they often belittle the camera check; they say that it's just semantic—or that it's just a word game—because I know what they really meant. And in part they are right; I usually do know what they meant. But, as

152

you'll soon find out, **one of the most common causes of irrational emotions, is saying what you don't mean and meaning what you don't say, but believing every word of it.** That's why it's so important to keep in mind that it really does make a difference how you describe external reality. Your thinking at A had a very different effect on you from your thinking at D-sub-a. Right?

Bob: That's true.

Dr. M.: What was that difference?

Bob: Well, the way I was thinking at A could get me into trouble.

Dr. M.: How did it make you feel?

Bob: Bad.

Dr. M.: Exactly. You felt angry. Right?

Bob: Yes, angry.

Dr. M.: But which thinking was more honest and factual about the lady—your first type or your second type?

Bob: The second.

Dr. M.: Exactly. But if you ignore that fact, you'll go around feeling chronically angry toward people; and at any given time you will be very likely to act angrily toward them. Right?

Bob: Right.

Dr. M.: And that could get you into trouble. Right?

Bob: That's right.

Dr. M.: Now, you might say, "Well, I'm not that kind of guy; I would never do anything to a poor, defenseless old lady." And I say, well, if that's the case, then all the more reason not to think in a way that keeps you angry at her. Anger puts an unnecessary emotional strain on you. It puts you in a situation that's like a person who lives in a house with a loose rattlesnake; but instead of killing the rattlesnake or moving out of the house, the person decides to become an expert on immediately knowing exactly where the rattlesnake is at any given second, so that he can protect himself from being bitten.

Bob: That reminds me of this Indian army buddy I had. He used to make jokes about how bad his Dad said living on the reservation used to be. He said some times the rattlers would move right in with them and they'd just make room.

Dr. M.: But that would put you in a tremendous emotional strain. And every four or five days you would probably want to go out and get drunk to unwind and relax. Right?

Bob: Yes. (Laughing)

Dr. M.: I see our time is up for this appointment. Put a check mark where we stopped, and we'll pick up there next session. Since this is your first RSA, I want to go over it with you slowly and thoroughly before you try to write another one. In the meantime you can practice on this AS-IF-RSA.*

---

*AS-IF-RSA's are partially done RSA's of real people's problems, that other people complete as if they were their problems. This self-technique was devised and tested at the RBT Center. For further information about AS-IF-RSA's write the RBT Center, College of Medicine, University of Kentucky, Lexington, Ky. 40506.

EMPHASIS QUESTIONS

1. A written _____ is an important aid for improved emotional self _____, and decreases _____ abuse.
2. Patients are encouraged to do an RSA at _____ time they are more upset than they _____ to be.
3. When therapists structure individual sessions around RSA's they first ask the patient to read the E section. True or False?
4. While discussing patients' RSA's, counselors look for reasons to reinforce patients. True or False?
5. RSA is only for really important problems. True or False?
6. Even trivial _____ may need _____ self-_____.
7. Many seemingly overwhelming problems turn out to be _____ of objectively _____ events.
8. There is no _____ thought, feeling or action that's too _____ to analyze _____.
9. Because Bob used to get drunk about the event in his RSA, it was worth an RSA. True or False?
10. When patients first begin to do RSA's they often take _____.
11. Shortcuts for doing RSA's rarely help people. True or False?
12. Neglecting to write the _____ Questions For _____ is a _____ short cut in doing _____.
13. Such patients (see item #12) usually don't really want to solve their problems. True or False?
14. Most people _____ with the five rules for rational thinking as soon as they _____ them.
15. You can use the five rational rules but still not think and behave rationally. True or False?

CORRECT ANSWERS

1. RSA, control, drug or alcohol
2. any, want
3. False
4. True
5. False
6. problems, rational, analysis
7. exaggerations, trivial
8. undesirable, trivial, rationally
9. True
10. shortcuts
11. True
12. Five, Rational, Thinking, common, RSA's
13. False
14. agree, hear
15. True

13

Why Your Attitude is the "IT" that Upsets You

Normally I start a counseling session by asking patients if they have an immediate problem to discuss. If they do, we discuss it. If they don't have one, and if there is an unfinished RSA from the prior session, we begin the present session where we stopped in the prior one.*

Dr. M.: Okay, Bob, the last session ended right after we went over the A section of your RSA about your "nosy" neighbor. If you don't have any more pressing problems today, let's pick up with your B-1 statement in that RSA.

Bob: Fine. My B-1 is: "She becomes very angry when I refuse to tell her such things as the company I keep all hours of the night." I put "bad" by that one.

Dr. M.: How did you challenge it?

---

*If there are no unfinished RSA's, we go over a new one or discuss other aspects of the patient's problem. Regardless of the topic of discussion, I structure the discussion around A, the facts, B, the patients' beliefs, C, the undesirable consequences of A and B, and what rational changes in A, B and C patients believe are best for them to make.

Bob: Let's see. Db-1: "She can't help but be angry at me about the loud company I keep all hours of the night. It would be very disturbing to anyone who is trying to sleep."

But Facts Don't Control Emotions

Bob's B and Db section statements both sounded like simple statements of fact. But facts neither make people angry nor stop them from getting angry. Instead, people's attitudes about facts trigger and stop their anger.

Why Admitting To Bad Attitudes Is Not Enough

By writing "bad" after his B-1 statement Bob showed he had a bad or negative attitude about it. **You can be sure his "bad" attitude was an angry one because his emotional reaction at C was anger.** But Bob neither challenged nor changed that angry attitude in his Db-1 debate. If B attitudes are neither challenged nor changed, they remain powerful and ready to trigger the same C reactions in similar, future situations.

To challenge and change their attitude rationally people must convert the attitude into its spoken or BELIEF form. Then they must check the belief with the Five Questions For Rational Thinking. That's what I helped Bob do next.

Dr. M.: Okay, that was a very good debate as far as it went. But I think it might have been better if you had pointed out to yourself that your B statement is a simple statement of fact. That's important to keep in mind because you ended up with unwanted anger at C. Right?
Bob: Right.
Dr. M.: But, we know that facts don't make people angry. It's their attitudes and beliefs about the facts that do it. But you neither described nor rationally debated your negative or bad attitude about what the lady did.
Bob: My attitude? I don't see what you are getting at.

158

Dr. M.: Okay, look at it like this. You said she gets angry when you refuse to answer her questions. Right?

Bob: Right.

Dr. M.: Okay. So what triggered your anger at C?

Bob: Her sticking her nose into my business.

Dr. M.: No, no, no. That's where you made your mistake. Your angry attitude about what she did triggered your anger. Now what did you think about what she did?

Bob: Well, most times, I didn't think anything. I mean I could just pick up the phone and hear her whining voice and it would just blow my mind.

Dr. M.: No, no, no. It didn't blow your mind. You blew your own mind with your angry attitude about the fact that she called. You see, your attitudes are the unspoken forms of your beliefs. Your attitudes make it unnecessary to think the words in your beliefs anymore; that's why you don't notice them. You just make a habitual perception and your attitudes trigger your habitual reactions instantly without your needing or even having time to think anything. It's all

	so quick; it's like a reflex. But you are still doing it. That's a very important insight; and you have to make it before you can discover which of your attitudes you must replace to stop making yourself angry in that type situation. Do you follow me so far?
Bob:	Well, (pause) sorta.

Bob seemed confused. But to quickly solve his problem with irrational anger, he needed to understand this point about attitudes and emotional control.

When I approach such therapeutic dead ends, I stop and retreat to a point where the patient and I can completely understand and agree with each other. Then, I slowly work back to the point of retreat. Such calm repetition almost always leads to efficient, therapeutic learning.

Irrational Should's
Trigger Irrational Anger

Dr. M.:	Look at it like this. Read your B sentence again.
Bob:	She becomes very angry when I refuse to talk to her about the company I keep all hours of the night.
Dr. M.:	All right, that's a simple statement of fact: she gets angry when you refuse to talk to her. Right?
Bob:	Right.
Dr. M.:	Okay, do you think that her behavior is a good thing for her to do or a bad thing?
Bob:	No, it's definitely wrong; she should mind her own business.
Dr. M.:	Oh, she should? In your opinion, that is.
Bob:	Right. What's wrong with that?
Dr. M.:	Nothing is wrong with it. I'm not saying there is anything wrong with it. I'm just trying to get you to see what attitude triggered your anger. It was your attitude that she shouldn't have been doing what she was doing. Right?
Bob:	Right. That's more or less what I was trying to put into words, but it seems more like a feeling than a thought.
Dr. M.:	That's right. And you were focused on your feelings; it was

	hard to put them into words because there were no words at that moment. You were reacting solely to your "should" attitude—that is, your unspoken belief that people "should not" stick their noses into your personal business.
Bob:	Right. That's definitely what I believe. Everybody should mind their own business.
Dr. M.:	So, when you mistakenly perceived that lady doing what she should not have been doing, BAM!, your "should-not" attitude instantly and automatically triggered your anger. You didn't have time to think anything; but you are so well programmed for anger in that situation, you didn't need to think to get angry.
Bob:	(visibly irritated) But how can you say I made a mistake? She really was nosing into my business.

When a patient's irritation is primarily caused by honest emotional ignorance such as Bob's was then, my strategy is still a calm retreat to the nearest point of complete understanding and agreement. Then I slowly work back to the point of confusion, using the everyday language of the patient.

Dr. M.:	Oh, I believe she did what she did. But your mistake was believing that she should not have done it. Your belief was a mistake because the obvious fact was that she should have done exactly what she did do. Do you follow that?
Bob:	(Pause) I think I do.
Dr. M.:	Okay, then explain it to me. Why do you think she should have done exactly what she did?
Bob:	(Pause, then smiles sheepishly) Wait a minute. I'm getting confused again.

Helpful Insights Are For The Patients

I know that I can't read patients' minds; so I don't try to. That's why to be sure patients understand the helpful insights I'm trying to teach them, I simply ask patients to explain those insights to me. If they can, THAT'S GREAT!! I quickly move on. But if patients can't explain them, I stop, retreat to a basic theoretical point on which we both agree, and slowly work forward.

Rational Shoulds Are Just Good English

Dr. M.: That's okay; don't be ashamed of it; in fact, admitting confusion is the first step toward rapid insight. Now let's see; what's the best way to make my point? Tell me, do you know the meaning of the word "shall?"

Bob: Shall (pause), ah, it means I will, or am going to do something.

Dr. M.: That's right, but it also has a more general meaning. Originally it meant "will have to" or "must," and it now means "is inevitable" or "seems likely to happen." Now, do you know what the relationship is between "should" and "shall"?

Bob: Hmm. You got me. English was never one of my strong points.

Dr. M.: Well, don't feel badly about not knowing that. Most Ph.D.'s in English either don't know it or they act as if they don't. But the fact is that "should" is the past tense of "shall." Did you realize that?

Bob: No, I don't think I ever heard that before.

Dr. M.: Okay, fine, but you do know what the "past tense" means. Right?

Bob: Yeah.

Dr. M.: Good! So since the original meaning of "shall" was "will have to," then "should" must have originally meant what?

Bob: Had to.

Dr. M.: Exactly. And in the modern meaning of shall "should" means "was inevitable," which is essentially the same as "had to be"; that's why in rational thinking we say everything is always exactly as it should be now, because "should" means "had to be" or "was inevitable." How can something be inevitable or how can something have to be and at the same time not be?

Bob: That can't be.

Dr. M.: Right. It's impossible. Okay, so do you see why if something does in fact exist now, it's a mistake to say it should not be? Do you see that?

Bob: Yeah, (pause) I think so.

Dr. M.: Okay, if you see that, then you can see why it was a mistake, for you to see that the lady was **not** minding her own business, and still believe she should have been minding it. Do you now agree to that?

Bob: (pause) Not really.

Again, my strategy was to retreat to a point of mutual agreement. The point of agreement I used here was: The mind through the

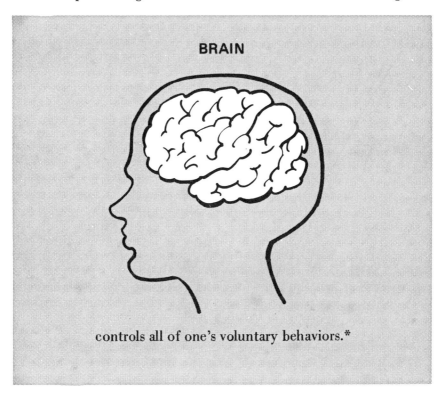

BRAIN

controls all of one's voluntary behaviors.*

Dr. M.: Okay, so far as we can tell, what controls everything I voluntarily do, you voluntarily do, and everything the little old lady voluntarily did and does?

Bob: You do; I mean, we do with our brains or mind.

---

*Problem drinkers who refuse to accept that fact are usually inappropriate for The New Self-Help Treatment of their drinking problem.

Dr. M.: Right. Now, is it possible to do anything voluntarily without our minds directing us to do it? So far as we know, that is?

Bob: (Long pause) No, I mean, you can think about doing something and then not do it; but your mind will have to stop directing you to do it, and will then be directing you not to do it. So your mind is still directing you.

Dr. M.: That's right. And because of that fact, will you agree that at the time the lady asked you about your personal affairs, her mind and brain were directing her to do it?

Bob: (Pause) Right.

Dr. M.: Okay. Now, could she have minded her own business in spite of the fact that her mind and brain were directing her not to mind it? I mean, could she at the same time do and not do what her mind and brain were directing her to do?

Bob: No, she couldn't.

Dr. M.: All right. Then it sounds to me as if the lady had to do what she did. Her mind and brain didn't allow her any other choice at that moment. To have acted differently, she would have had to have been thinking differently. But there is no reason to believe that she was thinking differently, right?

Bob: Right (with a big smile). She had to do it.

Dr. M.: Okay, do you see why I said you were mistaken when you thought she shouldn't have done it?

Bob: Yes, she should have done it?

Dr. M.: Exactly! So, the next time people ask you about your personal business, I think the most rational thoughts to have would be: "these people are asking me about my personal business and they probably are going to get angry when I ignore them; but if they do, that is exactly what they should do. I won't like it, but they should do it. But I don't have to get angry to prove to myself that I don't like something." Do you believe that?

Bob: Yeah, that's true. I don't have to get mad just because I don't like something.

Dr. M.: And it's equally true that you have no right to disturb your neighbors. So if you want them to stop asking about your activities, it probably would be a good idea for you to change your noisy habits starting today. Now, tell me, do these ideas make more rational sense to you than your old way of thinking?

Bob: They sure do.

Dr. M.: Are you willing to adopt these new ways of thinking and reacting?

Bob: That's exactly what I'm going to do.

Dr. M.: Good. Well, I see our time is up for today. So put a checkmark by B-2 so we will know where to start next week. But in the meantime, I want you to begin doing at least one RSA per week.

THE POWER OF RATIONAL THINKING

I especially like to emphasize the next point to physicians as well as patients: **for stopping irrational anger, there is no pill as fast or as safe as just repeating the next two sentences quickly and sincerely:**

The key word in this phrasing is now. Everything is as it should be now. It means, given the preceding conditions, the present situation was unavoidable and could not have been otherwise. When people ignore that fact, they control their emotions with their unrealistic should attitude (i.e., the unspoken belief) that their part of the world should be the way they want or demand it, regardless of the preceding conditions. But in the real world situations are produced by their preceding conditions. That's why those people have numerous opportunities to get irrationally angry.

But don't misunderstand me. **I'm not against anger. Anger is a powerful and useful emotion. When anger is rational** it prepares people physically and psychologically to defend themselves from probable danger, as well as to do what they can to change their part of the world to their desires.

The great reformers of the world often have been angry people. But the ones who did the most good with the least harm were usually just angry enough to work most effectively for the changes they wanted, without feeling angrier than they wanted to feel. That's rational anger; and answering the Five Questions For Rational Thinking is the best way to tell if you have it.

RATIONAL SHOULD'S AND SCIENCE

In spite of my lesson in correct English, a few chronically angry problem drinkers initially resist using rational shoulds. They usually pride themselves in being hard-headed scientific thinkers. So I point out to them that rational shoulds are the basis of all science. Scientific research would be a waste of time if anything could ever be a way it should not be. It's only because everything is always as it should be now that scientists can discover what preceding conditions made the present situations happen.

Finally, I challenge these resistant patients to think of an exception to the rational use of should. Usually after pondering futilely for a session or two, they begin to see the validity and emotional value of rational shoulds. Then I start responding to statements such as:

"Dr. Maultsby, I know I should have . . ." with "Oh no, based on your beliefs at the time, you should not have . . ."

ADVICE FOR BEGINNING COUNSELORS

Early in Rational Self-Counseling training, temporary therapeutic impasses due to patient ignorance and confusion are common. The best therapeutic strategy is almost always a calm retreat to a point of mutual factual agreement, followed by a friendly but theoretically valid re-explanation.

Remember, the psychosomatic learning theory of Rational Self-Counseling is as scientifically valid and clinically useful as most other medical theories. Take advantage of that fact; rely on the RSC theory the same way surgeons (or other medical specialists) rely on their theories.

Well-trained surgeons won't abandon their logically made diagnosis of appendicitis, merely because patients don't understand the word or don't like the idea. Similarly, well-trained Rational Behavior Therapists and Counselors usually won't abandon their logically derived therapeutic insights, merely because patients don't understand them or don't like them.

There are three situations, however, wherein **I will temporarily abandon a valid therapeutic insight:**

1. if the patient does not seem to understand the insight after hearing it explained at least twice with everyday type examples,

    OR

2. if patients seem too emotionally involved with a particular aspect of their problem to think clearly,

    OR

3. if patients say or appear to be thinking: "I don't care what you or anybody says, I just can't or won't accept that idea.

THE VALUE OF SYSTEMATIC REPETITION

No one can force patients to do therapeutic learning. It's a private, individual act, completely controlled by the patients. But by regularly scheduled listening to tape recordings of their own Rational Self-Counseling sessions, patients most quickly clear up confusion caused by emotional and psychological ignorance. In addition, listening to tape recorded sessions of other successfully treated patients (who had similar problems) helps resistant patients discover helpful therapeutic insights for themselves. **Usually patients most quickly benefit from self-discovered insights.** That's one of the main reasons written RSA's are so helpful.

RSA'S ARE NOT ABSOLUTELY NECESSARY

In fact, between 5 percent and 15 percent of my patients simply refuse to do them. That's right, they simply won't do them. But if such patients are completely voluntary and regularly keep their appointments, they will learn to help themselves. Next is my usual strategy for working with such patients.

Imagine such a patient coming to a fifth or sixth session complaining, "My boss chewed me out for nothing yesterday, and it really got to me; I just had to take a couple of quick ones to control myself".

I would probably say, "Okay, if you had done an RSA that would be your A section. Now, tell me how you felt at C in that situation. Now, tell me the thoughts you had during and after that event. Now, tell me how you would like to feel and act in similar situations in the future. Now let's discuss that situation rationally, starting with the camera check of A."

While discussing the ABC's of such patients' problems, I often write up the problem in the standard RSA format. When I do I give the patients my write-up to study between sessions.

That minor change in my usual RSA routine helps such patients learn Rational Self-Counseling just as effectively (but usually not as quickly) as most patients who do systematic written RSA's.

TAKE MOST ROADS THAT LEAD TO ROME

That means, I take almost any rational road to the Rome of alcoholic cure, i.e. HAPPILY STAYING ON THE WAGON.

WHAT IF PATIENTS STILL DON'T PROGRESS?

My research shows that to the extent that people can learn anything at all, they can usually learn to control themselves more rationally. So regardless of patients' problems, if they seem capable of any new learning but have done little or none after ten weekly sessions in three months, I recommend that they get in our Intensive Self-Help treatment program. (See Chapter 15).

EMPHASIS QUESTIONS

1. By writing "bad" after his B-1 statement, Bob revealed he had a _____ or negative _____ about his B idea.
2. An _____ negative attitude remains unchallenged and _____.
3. To tell for sure whether or not his negative attitude was _____ Bob first had to convert it to its spoken _____ form.
4. Facts don't make people angry. True or False?
5. Bob created his own anger with his _____ attitude.
6. When patients get confused, Dr. Maultsby usually just presses ahead with what he is saying. True or False?
7. _____ really is one of the royal roads to learning.
8. Bob's anger at his neighbor over the phone was triggered by his attitude. True or False?
9. Using rational shoulds is a _____ way of thinking for problem drinkers than using _____ shoulds.
10. The popular concepts of should and shouldn't are usually quite _____.
11. To see if patients understand him, Dr. Maultsby simply _____ patients to _____ what they understand.
12. If patients disagree with a potentially helpful idea, it's usually best to abandon the idea. True or False?
13. When patients refuse to accept a helpful insight into their problem, they often discover the insight for themselves while _____ to the tape of their session.
14. Everything is always exactly as it _____ be now.
15. Should is the _____ tense of _____.
16. Shall means will _____ to or is _____.
17. Therefore, should means _____ to or _____ inevitable.
18. Irrational shoulds and shouldn'ts describe people's _____ and _____ instead of obvious _____.
19. The rational should is the _____ should.
20. People who are often irrationally angry tend to give up trying to correct undesirable situations if they can't correct them immediately. True or False?

CORRECT ANSWERS

1. bad, attitude
2. unchecked, unchanged
3. rational, belief
4. True
5. angry
6. False
7. Repetition
8. True
9. better, irrational
10. irrational
11. asks, explains
12. False
13. listening
14. should
15. past, shall
16. have, inevitable
17. had, was
18. wants, demands, (or likes, dislikes), facts
19. scientific
20. True

14

From Drinking to Nondrinking Behavior

Problem drinking is one of the oldest man-made problems. **Yet, its simplest and most effective solution has been known as long as the problem itself: REFUSE THAT FIRST DRINK!**

Simply acting out those four little words would wipe out problem drinking instantly. But instead of being wiped out, American problem drinking is increasing and spreading. Yet what could be easier than refusing that first drink? It's just a matter of saying "No, thank you," and leaving one's hands at rest.

That act takes much less energy (and is therefore much easier) than saying "Yes, I will," and then lifting one's hands, picking up and drinking glass after glass of alcoholic drinks. Then, WHY DON'T PROBLEM DRINKERS REFUSE THAT FIRST DRINK? They don't because it's not their habit to react to alcohol that way.

SCIENCE AND HUMAN NATURE

People are creatures of habit. At any moment **people are most likely to do what they are in the habit of doing.** Without practice, therefore, they are least likely to act contrary to their well-established habits. That's because old habits don't just disappear; they must be extinguished and replaced. That requires time and active practice. Those facts are among the most well-established in human behavioral science. And the process of habit extinction and replacement is called behavioral re-education.

BEHAVIORAL RE-EDUCATION

It has FIVE STAGES and occurs in this order:

(1) Intellectual Insight
(2) Practice
    1. REI (Rational Emotive Imagery)
    2. Rational Real Life Practice
(3) Cognitive-Emotive Dissonance
(4) Emotional Insight
(5) New Personality Trait Formation

Intellectual insight means knowing and understanding the behaviors you must practice to achieve your desired emotive and physical re-education. Practice means repeatedly pairing the correct perceptions with the correct thoughts needed for the desired re-education to occur. The two forms of practice are self-explanatory, but **Cognitive-Emotive Dissonance** deserves detailed discussion.

Cognitive-Emotive Dissonance means having illogical emotive feelings about the perceptions, thoughts, and physical actions being experienced.

Problem drinkers experience Cognitive-Emotive Dissonance as an urge to drink even though they sincerely don't want to drink. Their environments, e.g. parties, bars, restaurants, etc. plus almost all of the outstanding features of those situations, e.g. listening to favorite party music, smoking, etc. are well-learned cues for strongly craving alcoholic drinks, even though the cured alcoholics sincerely don't want to drink. If they are not taught how to resist those cravings, most alcoholics give in to them and start drinking again.

This third stage in getting rid of habitual problem drinking seems unavoidable. That's why problem drinkers need to know how to recognize and handle it rationally; otherwise, they get confused and take running jumps off the wagon.

THE WISDOM OF NATURE

People cannot change their habitual gut or emotive feelings as fast as they can change their minds. That's why Cognitive-Emotive Dissonance is probably unavoidable; and it's probably fortunate that it is. Otherwise many people might accidentally kill themselves.

Noticeable gut or emotive feelings result from changes in the current interactions of the vital organ systems. To maintain good health, those interactions must remain at or near a homeostatic state most of the time. That's why many people would die if they could make their gastro-intestinal, cardiovascular, and genito-urinary systems change their interactions as wildly as they can make their thoughts change.

Think of how worn out most people are after three hours of diarrhea. Then, only one vital organ system is deviating wildly from normal; and people sometimes die from that.

In light of those medical facts, it's easy to see why rational behavioral scientists believe Cognitive-Emotive Dissonance may have a self-protective function. Whether or not that's a fact has not been proven. But over a half million dollars in research on behavioral re-education in problem and nonproblem drinkers indicates that people almost never replace a habit without experiencing some Cognitive-Emotive Dissonance.

Emotional insight means having logical emotional feelings for the perceptions, thoughts, and physical actions being practiced.

Personality trait formation means developing semipermanent behavioral units called habits. Habits consist of attitudes or beliefs and repeatedly associated emotive and physical actions. Habits form automatically through continued practice.

Forming new personality traits indicates that re-education is relatively complete and semipermanent. But, by resuming old habits or by learning new ones, people can easily replace new personality traits. That's why problem drinkers need to continue their newly learned Rational Self-Counseling the rest of their lives.

TEACHING PATIENTS ABOUT HABIT RE-EDUCATION

Usually the more useful the understanding people have about their re-educational tasks, the easier and faster they complete the tasks rationally. Most problem drinkers understand the process of driver re-education. Since all re-education seems to occur in the **same five stages, I use driver re-education as the example to teach problem drinkers the five stages involved in learning how to refuse that first drink.**

Imagine that you are a lifelong American auto driver, but today you will fly to England and start driving English cars. In England driving instruments are on the car's right-hand side, and English traffic proceeds on the left-hand side of roads. Therefore, to drive safely in England you must give yourself a driver re-education. But since you now understand about English cars and traffic, you already have intellectual insight into your task of driver re-education.

Now, imagine yourself at the busy London International Airport. There you sit on the right-hand side of your English car, driving off on the left-hand side of the busy English roads. **How do you imagine you would feel emotionally?**

All of my patients have immediately imagined correctly. They'd feel "ODD, STRANGE, or SCARED," as if "This is all wrong." They are sure they'd feel that way, even though they would know they would be driving correctly.

That, I explain, would be Cognitive-Emotive Dissonance. Your mind would be directing you in the correct driving reactions for safe English driving, but your gut or emotive feelings would make you feel as if the correct way were really incorrect.

Without exception, my patients also clearly see that:

(1) To complete their driver re-education, they would have to ignore their inappropriate gut feelings and let their minds and brains direct them with correct perceptions and correct thoughts and actions for English driving.

(2) Even though they were to drive correctly from the airport to their hotel, that one correct performance would not mean they had completed their driver re-education.

(3) There would be no way of knowing beforehand how long it would take them to get emotional insight into English driving and thereby complete the major part of their driver re-education. But they know it will take as long as it takes.

They also know that if they practiced correct English driving daily, they would complete their re-education as quickly as possible for them.

Then I explain, those three facts apply equally as well to replacing the habit of taking that first drink with the new habit of refusing it. **Before problem drinkers can realistically expect to refuse that first drink instantly and consistently without contrary feelings, they must practice doing it.** Traditional alcoholic treatment programs don't give problem drinkers that practice. That is one of the reasons such treated alcoholics repeatedly jump off the wagon.

Normally, neither problem drinkers, nor their friends, nor their counselors associate practice with refusing that first drink. Consequently, even though they all understand the example of driver re-education, they usually don't see how to apply those insights to learning to refuse that first alcoholic drink.

Out of ignorance, therefore, most problem drinkers (as well as their friends and counselors) naively confuse the interruptions in their habitual problem drinking (caused by traditional alcoholic treatment programs) with having extinguished their habitual problem drinking. Unfortunately, confusion does not change the facts that **interruptions in problem drinking (such as caused by jail or hospitalization) are just that—interruptions, but not habit extinction.**

Granted, a few problem drinkers probably can and do swear off alcohol for the first and only time and never go back to it. And a few American drivers probably can go to England and drive perfectly from day one. But in either case, the number is so small it would be absurd to expect any specific person to do it.

Without prolonged, frequent practice, the most rational expectation is that almost all new American drivers in England would have dangerous slips back into their old American driving habits; and even after prolonged practice, some would still slip back a few times. But with reasonable amounts of initial driver re-education and practice, most new American drivers in England don't make dangerous slips back into American driving habits; and they usually stop making such slips altogether much quicker than they would without initial driver re-education and practice. The same behavioral facts apply equally well to other habits, including the habit of refusing to take that first drink. That fact makes nondrinking practice an important part of the New Self-Help Treatment of alcoholics and problem drinkers.

DAILY NONDRINKING PRACTICE

Twice per day we have our patients sit at a table alone in front of two empty glasses, a bottle of their favorite alcoholic drink and a bottle of their favorite soft drink or juice. Then several times while listening to a recording of our standard nondrinking lecture, patients look at, smell, and handle their alcoholic drink; but they refuse to drink it.

After patients are comfortable doing that practice maneuver, we send them to local bars alone and in small patient groups. That practice routine achieves two important goals.

1. It teaches problem drinkers that they can enjoy themselves in the presence of alcohol without drinking.

2. It enables problem drinkers to extinguish their habitual problem drinking in the most realistic setting possible—the real world of alcohol at every turn.

EMPHASIS QUESTIONS

1. The most effective _____ to problem drinking has been known as long as there has been problem drinking.
2. _____ that _____ drink is the most effective solution to problem drinking.
3. Problem drinkers don't refuse that first drink because they just can't do it. True or False?
4. People are creatures of _____.
5. You don't just _____ up a _____; you replace it with another one.
6. There are at least _____ stages in behavioral _____.
7. The five steps in behavioral re-education are:
   (1) _____
   (2) _____
   (3) _____
   (4) _____
   (5) _____
8. Intellectual insight simply means _____ what you have to _____ to achieve your re-education.
9. Practice is essential for re-education to occur. True or False?
10. Cognitive-Emotive Dissonance proves that gut feelings are the best guide for making decisions. True or False?
11. Cognitive-Emotive Dissonance leads you to do what you _____ is wrong and makes you _____ right doing it.
12. Cognitive-Emotive Dissonance is unavoidable in behavioral re-education. True or False?
13. Emotional insight proves that gut thinking is superior to brain thinking. True or False?
14. Emotional insight merely means _____ gut _____ that are _____ for your _____.
15. If alcohol counselors know what they are doing, they can tell problem drinkers exactly how many weeks or months they will need to re-educate themselves. True or False?
16. It _____ as long as it _____ for habitual problem drinkers to learn to solve their drinking problem.
17. It's really unfortunate that people can't change their guts as fast as they can change their minds. True or False?

CORRECT ANSWERS

1. solution
2. Refusing, first
3. False
4. habit
5. give, habit
6. five, re-education
7. Intellectual Insight
   Practice
   Cognitive-Emotive
      Dissonance
   Emotional Insight
   New Personality
      Trait Formation
8. knowing, practice
9. True
10. False
11. know, feel
12. True
13. False
14. having, feelings, logical, thoughts
15. False
16. takes, takes
17. False

PLEASE NOTE

The STANDARD NONDRINKING RECORDED LECTURE mentioned on pages 178 and 197 is available for $8.95 (plus $1.00 postage and packaging) from The RBT Center, College of Medicine, University of Kentucky, Lexington, Ky., 40506.

SECTION III

The following chapters tie together the multitude of facts, insights, and rational strategies for helping problem drinkers help themselves stop drinking in the shortest time possible. And since prevention is the best long-term treatment of all, Chapter 18 ends this book by describing evidence that teaching Rational Self-Counseling in schools seems to be a practical and economical approach to preventing habitual alcohol abuse among teen-agers and adults.

    Chapter 15 The Intensive New Self-Help Alcoholic Treatment Program
    Chapter 16 Nondrinking Tape Scripts
    Chapter 17 Subtle Habits That Maintain Problem Drinking
    Chapter 18 Rational Self-Counseling To Prevent Alcohol Abuse

15

The Intensive New Self-Help Alcoholic Treatment Program

The permanent solution to problem drinking is behavioral re-education in the three drinking-related behaviors: cognitive, emotive, and physical. Problem drinkers can get that re-education in three ways: in in-patient treatment programs; once to three times per week out-patient treatment programs; and eight hours per day, ten to fifteen-day intensive out-patient treatment programs.

My staff and I specialize in eight hours per day, ten to fifteen-day intensive out-patient treatment programs. Such programs give problem drinkers the advantage of maximal behavioral re-education at the least total cost in time and money.

This chapter describes the daily schedule for our intensive treatment program. Where indicated, brief detailed descriptions explain the unique features of our treatment program.

―――――――― Schedule for the First Week ――――――――

MONDAY

8:00 - 9:00   Registration and Testing

We give two types of tests: standardized personality tests and our own YIPE (Your Irrational Potential Estimate).* The standard personality tests give us a general overview of the mental health status of a problem drinker. The YIPE scores tell us which specific irrational attitudes and beliefs may be triggering the emotional conflicts the problem drinker has been trying to wash away with alcohol.

9:00 - 10:00 Orientation
10:00 - 11:00 Initial interview with the primary therapist

Each problem drinker has a primary (senior staff) therapist and one or more co-therapists. During the initial interview (co-therapist may or may not be present) the primary therapist has three major goals:
  (1) to get enough data for an accurate mental health diagnosis;
  (2) to define up to three of the patient's most significant emotional conflicts;
  (3) to discover the patient's main cognitive habits.

The label "most significant emotional conflicts" refers to emotional conflicts that have these three features:
  (1) They are problems that the problem drinkers (and their spouses**) are willing to work on in the intensive treatment program.
  (2) They are problems that the problem drinkers can effectively deal with during the intensive treatment program.
  (3) By solving these problems, the problem drinkers will be more satisfied with their daily lives without alcohol than they have been with it.

---

*See Page 224.
**If a problem drinker is living with a significant-other (spouse, relative, friend) whose life is influenced significantly by the problem drinker's behavior, we advise the significant-other to go through the intensive re-education program with the problem drinker. Even though the significant-others do not have significant emotional problems themselves, our self-help program still helps them very much. It teaches them how to interact in the most helpful way with their problem-drinking mates. That frees the problem drinkers and their significant-others to work at strengthening and improving their usually strained or damaged relationship.

In my clinical experience patients usually don't work effectively on more than three significant problems at any one time. By restricting patients to three or fewer problems per week, they usually develop skill in rational problem solving in the shortest time possible. Such patients are most likely to continue their Rational Self-Counseling after they return home.

Cognitive habits refers to how patients usually perceive and think about themselves and the outside world, especially when faced with stress. Irrational cognitive habits often form mental smoke screens that prevent patients from clearly defining their problems.

The six such common irrational cognitive habits are:

(1) Abusing generalities; for example, the inaccurate use of ALWAYS and NEVER.

(2) Often saying "I CAN'T" when they really mean, "I'm afraid," "I refuse," or "I just don't want to."

(3) Often frightening themselves with improbable "What if's"; for example, refusing to apply for a job because "What if I just make a complete mess of everything" or "What if I really hate everybody who works there?"

(4) Often giving, "yes, but" agreements that seem to justify ignoring obvious, easy solutions to their problems. For example, in response to: "You could let your teenagers clean their own rooms," a self-harrassed problem drinking mother might say: "Yes, you are right, but I just can't stand the thought of a junkyard in my house."

(5) Often listening to other people but hearing only themselves listening. For example, you might say: "But you don't have to get drunk every day just because your marriage is breaking up." The patients may respond with, "But I have got real feelings."

No, that doesn't mean those patients are schizophrenic. It's just that they will have heard me say, "You don't have to get drunk everyday just because your marriage is breaking up." Then in their heads these patients will have thought something like, "You would have to be an unfeeling robot to be totally unconcerned about your marriage breaking up. He must think I don't have any feelings." Their last idea ("He must think I don't have any feelings") is what they read into what I said. And they responded to that with, "But I've got real feelings," instead of responding to what I actually said.

(6) Frequent irrational emotive imagery. For example, Dr. Ryan often pictured himself about to be attacked. But in fact he had only received an unwanted order, about which he got as angry as he would have been in a fight. That's what often led him to act like a Rebel-Without-A-Cause.

11:00 - 12:00 First group meeting

The primary emphasis is on getting acquainted with the other group members. As the patients talk, the group leader emphasizes the similarities in their thought patterns and in their nonalcohol-induced problems.

CORRECTING THE SPECIAL BREED MYTH

Problem drinkers usually have the incorrect belief that they are a special breed of human being or that they have a uniquely unbearable cross. To quickly correct that self-defeating idea, we mix our problem drinkers in with our patients receiving intensive self-help treatment for nondrinking problems. Usually before the group meeting is half over every participant has seen some dimension of his or her problems in the problem spectrum of someone else. Invariably, patients with drinking problems find that experience reassuring, self-enlightening, and encouraging.

12:00 - 1:00	Lunch
1:00 - 1:45	Individual treatment session. This meeting focuses on how emotions work. Patients call this session "Learning Your Emotional ABC's".
1:45 - 2:00	Break
2:00 - 5:00	Rational Group Encounter.* Patients continue their discussion of emotions and learn the five rules for rational behavior.
5:00 - 6:00	Dinner
6:00 - 7:30	Rational Group Encounter. Patients learn the concept and format of Rational Self-Analysis (RSA).

OVERNIGHT ASSIGNMENT

Patients write a Rational Self-Analysis of a past personal event that has usually ended in their getting drunk. They also do assigned rational self-help readings for the therapeutic material covered during the day.

By 8:00 a.m. the second day patients will have had the equivalent therapeutic exposure of 6-8 weeks in once-per-week out-patient treatment programs.

TUESDAY

8:30 - 9:30   Instructional videotape session

---

*These groups are really intensive, classroom-type seminars on the basic facts and techniques in Rational Self-Counseling.

Because treatment without drugs is really behavioral re-education, most effective learning aids facilitate the process. Instructional videotapes are one of our favorite self-help learning aids. Our instructional tapes (valued at over $100,000.00) show real people using RSC to solve personal problems similar to those of our patients. This therapeutic activity helps us maximally intensify the re-educational experience.

9:30 - 11:30   Rational Self-Counseling Group

Humans seem to be basically social beings; that's probably why most types of learning occur best in internally reinforcing small group settings. Our intensive program includes two or more small learning experiences per day.

11:00 - 12:00   Individual treatment session
12:00 - 1:00   Lunch
 1:00 - 3:00   Personalized self-help assignments

Such an assignment may be viewing and doing a personalized analysis of an instructional videotape; it may be listening to a tape of one's own individual treatment session; or it may be a behavioral assignment away from the Medical Center. For example, we send our patients to bars to practice enjoying themselves there while drinking only soft drinks.

3:00 - 5:00   Rational Self-Counseling Group*

OVERNIGHT ASSIGNMENT

Write at least one Rational Self-Analysis and begin Rational Emotive Imagery. Do assigned rational self-help reading for therapeutic material covered during the day.

WEDNESDAY

8:30 - 9:30   Individual treatment session. All of these sessions are audiotaped. Depending upon the patients' apparent needs, we often videotape these sessions.
9:30 - 11:00   Rational Self-Counseling Group
11:00 - 12:00 Individual session
12:00 - 1:00   Lunch
1:00 - 3:00   Personalized self-help (same as Tuesday)
3:00 - 5:00   Rational self-counseling group

OVERNIGHT ASSIGNMENT

Same as Tuesday

THURSDAY

8:30 - 9:30   Instructional videotape and discussion.**
9:30 - 11:00   Rational Self-Counseling Group
11:00 - 12:00 Individual session
12:00 - 1:00   Lunch
1:00 - 3:00   Personalized self-help. This will include editing a non-drinking script to make it personally appropriate for one's own self. Later that person will record that script in his or her own voice (see Chapter 16).
3:00 - 5:00   Rational Self-Counseling Group

---

*This is the typical therapeutic rational self-help group. The group is led by a trained Rational Behavior Group Therapist.

**Therapist or co-therapist leads these discussions.

OVERNIGHT ASSIGNMENT

Same as Tuesday

FRIDAY

 8:30 - 9:30 Instructional videotape and discussion
 9:30 - 11:00 Rational Self-Counseling Group
11:00 - 12:00 Individual treatment sessions
12:00 - 1:00 Lunch
 1:00 - 2:00 Personal self-help work on assignments. Recording and listening to personalized nondrinking script.
 2:00 - 3:15 Rational Self-Counseling Group
 3:30 - 4:00 Individual treatment session.
 4:00 - 5:00 End of week party (soft drinks ONLY, with ice cream and/or cake, and rational fun)

WEEKEND ASSIGNMENT

With the help of their therapists and the group members, each patient will have developed behavioral assignments to be carried out over the weekend. Patients analyze in writing their weekend performances or their refusals to perform their assigned tasks. During the next week they present those RSA's in their individual and group sessions.

──────────── **Schedule for the Second Week** ────────────

MONDAY

 8:30 - 9:30 Go out and buy a bottle of your favorite alcoholic drink and your favorite non-alcoholic drink.
 9:30 - 11:00 Rational Self-Counseling Group. Discuss morning assignment and weekend activities.
11:00 - 12:00 Individual treatment session
12:00 - 1:30 Lunch
 1:30 - 2:30 Personal self-help work assignments. Same as above.

2:30 - 3:00 Nondrinking practice session.* (See Chapter 16)
3:00 - 5:00 Rational Self-Counseling Group
5:00 - 5:30 Nondrinking practice session

OVERNIGHT ASSIGNMENT

Same as last Thursday plus any individualized behavioral assignments.

TUESDAY

8:00 - 8:30 Nondrinking practice session
8:30 - 9:30 Instructional videotape session and discussion
9:30 - 11:00 Rational Self-Counseling Group
11:00 - 12:00 Individual treatment session
12:00 - 12:30 Nondrinking practice session
12:30 - 1:30 Lunch
1:30 - 2:30 Self-help work assignments
2:30 - 3:00 Nondrinking practice session
3:00 - 5:00 Rational Self-Counseling Group
5:00 - 5:30 Nondrinking practice session

OVERNIGHT ASSIGNMENT

Same as Monday plus nondrinking session at home (or in motel room for out-of-town patients).**

WEDNESDAY AND THURSDAY

8:00 - 8:30 Nondrinking practice session
8:30 - 9:30 Instructional videotape and discussion

---

*Therapist or co-therapist is available for discussion of reaction to these sessions.
**Over half of our intensive treatment patients are from out of state.

9:30 - 11:00	Rational Self-Counseling Group
11:00 - 12:00	Individual treatment session
12:00 - 12:30	Nondrinking practice session
12:30 - 1:30	Lunch
1:30 - 2:30	Self-help assignments
2:30 - 3:00	Nondrinking practice session
3:00 - 5:00	Rational Self-Counseling Group
5:00 - 5:30	Nondrinking practice session

OVERNIGHT ASSIGNMENT

Same as above.

THURSDAY

8:00 - 8:30	Nondrinking practice session
8:30 - 9:30	Instructional videotape and discussion
9:30 - 11:00	Rational Self-Counseling Group
11:00 - 12:00	Individual treatment session
12:00 - 12:30	Nondrinking practice session
12:30 - 1:30	Lunch
1:30 - 2:30	Personal self-help work assignments
2:30 - 3:00	Nondrinking practice session
3:00 - 5:00	Rational Self-Counseling Group
5:00 - 5:30	Nondrinking practice session
5:30 -	End of week party

OVERNIGHT SESSION

Same as above.

WEEKEND ASSIGNMENT

With the help of therapists and group members, each patient will have developed behavioral assignments to be done over the weekend. This will include five extinction runs (see Chapter 14) each day at home or in the motel.

DAILY HOME-LIFE PLAN

The third week is essentially the same as the second except for one important new experience: Daily Home-Life Plans. Those are patients' personal plans for transferring their newly learned therapeutic insights and rational self-help maneuvers to their home, work, and social situation.

Each daily plan is a specific application of the general program for rationally handling known past stimuli for alcoholic drinking without alcohol.

Patients usually spend at least two hours daily (starting on Wednesday) working on their Daily Home-Life Plan under the direction of their therapists.

The above three weeks is the typical routine for the average patient. But we treat all our patients as individuals. That is why each is able to progress at his or her best pace.

The staff evaluates each patient's progress daily. Each Thursday each patient gets an individualized treatment recommendation for the coming week.

FOLLOW-UP CARE

Our intensive program teaches problem drinkers all they need to know to stay sober. But three weeks is not enough time to completely replace all their tendencies to jump off the wagon; that requires more time and continuous practice than just three weeks. And recently-cured alcoholics usually practice best under the instructive eye of a professional; therefore, we refer our patients back to their referring professionals. When there is no referring professional, we recommend one of the following after-care plans:

(1) We put patients in contact with an appropriately trained professional in their communities.
(2) When no appropriate professional is available in the patient's community, we set up a therapy-by-phone program for them.
   The phone bill for a thirty minute RSA session by phone between Lexington and Los Angeles after 5:00 p.m. is less than $6.00.
(3) We refer them to a rational self-help group in their home town.*

RETURN TO DRINKING

Many of our former patients experiment with some type of alcoholic beverage at least once within six months of completing our program. In our experience men are far more likely to report experimenting than women. In both cases, however, their main motivation seems to be continued preoccupation with proving the obvious: namely, that they can drink socially IF THEY ACTUALLY DRINK SOCIALLY—that is, if they stop before they feel the effects of the alcohol. The following excerpt from a former patient's letter summarizes the typical patient's experience.

---

*Rational Self-help groups are usually run by mental health professionals who have been trained at the RBT Center, College of Medicine, University of Kentucky, Lexington, Kentucky 40506.

"Doc, my wife and I are continuing to improve on our skills in rational self-control, learned in your program. Because of that, we are enjoying our marriage more than either of us can remember. I've been completely abstinent for the past year except for two times when I drank socially just to prove I could do it.

"I know you are probably thinking that I'm just fooling myself, that I've done that before and it's just a matter of time before I'll be drinking like a fish again. But I disagree because of these two rational reasons:

"First, I had never used the social drinker's stop light before. I used it both times this time.

"Second, I drank just to prove my point to myself, not the world. I do not intend to try to keep drinking socially. I'm still committed to staying on the wagon. But, like you said, it's not good for me to be afraid of alcohol; it can't do anything to me unless I force it to do it. Incidentally, stepping off the wagon is a HELL OF A LOT MORE FUN than jumping off."

WE ADMIT THE OBVIOUS

Complete abstinence is usually the best initial treatment goal of most problem drinkers. That's why abstinence is the main treatment goal of the New Intensive Self-Help Alcoholic Treatment Program. But **our patients** are usually well read, knowledgeable people. They **usually know about the Rand Report** and other research studies that prove some problem drinkers can learn to drink socially. Consequently, if problem drinkers are determined to re-learn social drinking skills, we will teach them.

SOCIAL DRINKING IS NOT FOR EVERY PROBLEM DRINKER

So far the research shows that the number of problem drinkers who succeed at social drinking is too small to make social drinking a routine initial treatment goal. That's why **we evaluate each potential social drinker individually.** Our main selection standard is at least six months of personally satisfying sober living, after their new Self-Help Alcoholic Treatment program. Briefly, the Training Center for Rational Behavior Therapy and Emotional Self-Help takes the position that:

MANY COULD, BUT FEW WILL

I view social drinking for most cured alcoholics the way I view winning the Kentucky Derby. Theoretically, every jockey could do it. But practically speaking, only a few actually will. It would be absurd, therefore, to tell every apprentice jockey, "You will win the Kentucky Derby." I think it would be equally absurd to tell every problem drinker, "You will learn to drink socially." At the Training Center for Rational Behavior Therapy and Emotional Self-Help, we tell problem drinkers, "First, we will teach you how to stop your problem drinking. After you achieve that goal, if you are **interested,** we will evaluate you for the likelihood of learning social drinking."

16

Nondrinking Tape Scripts

No one can lecture with more sincere personal feelings about the evils of alcohol abuse than hungover problem drinkers on the morning after. But it's a waste of time to have such thoughts then. All the bottles are empty. That's why NONDRINKING PRACTICE is an important part of the New Self-Help Alcoholic Treatment Method. It teaches problem drinkers to have nondrinking thinking at the most helpful time—WHEN THE BOTTLES ARE STILL FULL.

In our nondrinking practice sessions patients first listen to our standard, nondrinking, tape recorded lecture. Next they listen to our standard nondrinking script, after they have recorded it in their own voice.

OUR STANDARD NONDRINKING, RECORDED LECTURE

This is a composite case history of two successfully treated alcoholics. The recording was professionally done in the first person, as if one of the real alcoholics were telling his personal case history on tape.

The recording summarizes the main points problem drinkers need to remember to benefit most quickly from the New Self-Help Treatment Method. In addition, the tape reviews how to extinguish habitual problem drinking, avoid confusion and frustration, and STAY on the wagon.

When this tape is over, patients immediately listen to their own voice-recording of their individualized version of our standard nondrinking script (presented below), or they listen to a similar script they will have written for themselves.

OUR STANDARD NONDRINKING SCRIPT*

That's the most sensible talk I have ever heard about alcoholism. He sure is right about that first drink. If I don't drink it, I can't get drunk. The bottle sure looks good. I feel like I want to take a drink right now. But that's an irrational feeling. The facts are: I really don't want a drink; I really want to stop drinking. That's just my old secondary craving making me feel as if I want a drink. But I understand now that my craving is not my want. My want is to stop drinking. So I will just ignore my stupid craving and think with my mind and brain; then the craving will have to disappear fast.

I now see the big difference between wanting a drink and craving a drink. A want is just an idea; it exists only in my mind. That's why I can create and get rid of a want as fast as I can change my mind. But a craving is a feeling inside of my body. Until I extinguish my habit of craving, I will sometimes crave a drink, even though I don't want one. But if I refuse to support my craving with drinking-type thinking, the craving will quickly disappear. And if I do nondrinking practice daily, soon I will completely extinguish my habit of craving. But, like most worthwhile traits, it will take time and practice to learn not to crave alcohol. That's logical. I practiced for years to teach my body to crave alcohol; so I can't rationally expect to stop it overnight.

Fortunately, my mind still controls me; and it tells me that I don't want a drink, I don't need a drink, and I refuse to take a drink. I'll just follow my mind and instead of drinking alcohol, I'll take a drink of (read in the name of your favorite nonalcoholic drink or juice and take a swallow).

I used to think it was hard for me to refuse a drink. Now I see that it's really easy. All I have to do is follow my rational thoughts; that simple act will always make my craving go away without my taking a drink. All I have to do is ignore my craving and refuse that first drink just one more time than I get the urge to drink it, and I'll have it made.

---

*I, Maxie C. Maultsby, Jr., M.D., give my permission for anyone to record this script for his or her own non-profit, personal use in overcoming a personal drinking problem.

Hey! My stupid craving has started to go away already. That guy on that other tape was right. By just taking my mind off my craving and thinking rationally, I can make it go away fast. What could be easier than that?

It's really great to know that I really control me. I don't have to be a slave to a bottle anymore. I have a good mind. And I am going to use it to retrain my stupid gut. I don't want a drink, I don't need a drink, and I will refuse to take a drink. Instead, I will drink some nice cold (read in the name of your soft drink or juice and take a swallow).

This is really great! I can feel myself getting over my drinking problem already. Now I can honestly start thinking about what I can do for myself and my family.

First off, when I start to get **mad, bored, depressed,** or in anyway **upset,** I will refuse to drink to feel better. Instead, I will just turn on my rational thinking and honestly tell myself that I don't want to drink, I don't need to drink, and I refuse to take a drink. Drinking doesn't really help me; that's why it's stupid to keep on doing it. I don't have to drink to get un-upset. Now that I have learned Rational Self-Counseling, I see that I can feel as good as I want to, with just rational thinking. That's why I don't want a drink, I don't need a drink, and I refuse to take a drink.

Instead of drinking, when I start thinking that I'm worthless and no good I'll just call the friendly undertaker and check on the price of my funeral. That'll show me that I'm worth at least several hundred dollars to him. If I'm worth that much to a stranger after I'm dead, I'm certainly smart enough to be worth more than that to me while I'm alive.

It's just irrational self-pity that makes me feel as if I'm no damn good. But in reality, I know I am as good as anybody. I've just had the stupid habit of drinking more than most people. But now I'm on the road to getting rid of that stupid habit; I'm refusing that first drink and feeling good about doing it. That's really a new experience for me; but I like it; that's why I'm going to keep on doing it.

It's as easy to stop drinking as it is to stop smoking. I see that now. All I have to do is just refuse that first drink just one more time than I see it. This is easier than I ever dreamed. I don't want a drink, I don't need a drink, and I refuse to take a drink.

I don't care how my stupid gut feels. I have a brain and a rational mind. And I'm going to follow my rational mind and ignore my cravings. That guy on the tape was right; by just taking my mind off my cravings, I can make them go away. I have just proven for myself how easy it is to refuse that first drink. All I have to do is think straight and concentrate on what I really want, instead of what my stupid gut feeling has been tricking me into believing I want. I don't want a drink, I don't need a drink, and I will refuse to take a drink. Instead, I will take a drink of my nice cold (name your soft drink or juice and take a swallow). That's all I need anyway. This is really great!

No more (Read in whatever has been the undesirable results of your drinking; for example, no more hangovers or Monday, Tuesday, or Wednesday morning shakes). No more embarrassing myself and my family and friends. All I have to do is keep my thinking straight and I'll have it made. I'll have my self-respect again, and I won't ever have to be ashamed of me again. I'll be able to look any person in the eye and honestly say "I'm O.K. now; how about you?"

All I have to do is just stay with the facts, the whole facts, and nothing but the facts. And the facts are that I don't want a drink, I don't need a drink, and I refuse to take a drink. I'm going to enjoy my nice, cold (read the name of your soft drink or juice and take a swallow) and feel good about doing it."

Several times while listening to their voice recordings, patients stop their tapes and do REI, picturing themselves in past situations where they have habitually taken that first drink. But now they picture themselves thinking their rational thoughts and refusing alcoholic drinks.

Even after problem drinkers are no longer receiving formal training in Rational Self-Counseling, I recommend that they continue the daily nondrinking practice sessions at home for at least six months.

UNIQUELY PERSONAL NONDRINKING SCRIPTS

Some people prefer a more uniquely personal nondrinking script instead of our standard one. That's great! We encourage and help such patients write their own scripts. The more accurately a nondrinking script describes the personal thought patterns of individual problem drinkers, the less reason they have to ignore the script, and the more powerfully the nondrinking ideas will influence their nondrinking behavior.

Below is Dr. Ryan's personally written script. Notice that he began it by objecting to being lumped together with "all" problem drinkers. The more problem drinkers insist on seeing themselves or their problem as being unique, the more likely they are to want to write and follow their own nondrinking scripts.

DR. RYAN'S NONDRINKING SCRIPT

When I listen to that guy on the other tape, I get somewhat put off by a few of the things he says that seem to me to be like preaching. At those times he just doesn't ring true to me. He lumps all people with drinking problems together, as if they are all the same. I object to his referring to me as being an alcoholic, just like him. Though I am quite willing to admit to having a bit of a drinking problem, I am not like him. I am me. Just because I have one stupid behavior that he had, that doesn't make me an alcoholic like he was. He can't know how I feel or think.

Enough of that, though. I'm not going to waste my time on negatives. I'll focus on the helpful ideas he had. It was especially helpful to hear him explain the important difference between a want and a craving. I want things in my mind with my thoughts. That means my wanting is just my idea that I might like to have something. A craving is a feeling, actually an urge, that people train their bodies to have by continually giving themselves the addictive drugs they want.

There are three steps involved there:

First step. I want something, but that's just an idea that I have.

Second step. I give myself what I want. But if what I want and give myself is an addictive chemical like cigarettes or alcohol, and I keep on using it, my body gets dependent on interacting with it. As a doctor, I know that when your body gets dependent on a chemical, you feel upset when your body starts to lose it. That brings me to the third step.

Third step. Getting withdrawal symptoms when I don't get the chemical.

So by wanting and drinking alcohol over and over I have trained my body to crave it. And my craving or getting upset when I stop drinking has been the main force that has kept me in the habit of drinking.

But at first when I was a social drinker, I didn't crave alcohol. It was only by drinking too much too often for too many years that I trained my body to crave alcohol. And once I had learned to crave, my craving just kept my habit going. That's because my craving made me feel as if I wanted to drink more than was good for me to drink. And I easily got confused because when it came to drinking, I used to think with my gut instead of my brain; that's why I never said, "No, don't," when my cravings said, "Yes, take another drink." From now on, though, things will be different. I have rationally made up my mind about drinking. I don't want to drink anymore. Instead, I honestly and sincerely want to stop drinking.

But most important, I now see that in spite of my sincere desire to stop drinking, a few weeks from now when I would normally hang one on, I will probably get my old craving feelings and start feeling like I want and need a drink. I say "probably" because if I do my nondrinking practice three times a day as I plan to do now, I just may be able to extinguish my old cravings completely before it's time for my next bender.

But realistically speaking, I probably will get at least some mild cravings sometimes, for at least a little while longer. That's because I have trained my body to crave a drink whenever I even see, smell, or think about one. And because my gut doesn't have a brain, it will keep on making me feel as if I want and need a drink for a little while, even though I have already honestly stopped wanting a drink.

My rational mind tells me I don't want to drink; so I'll just keep on reminding myself that my cravings are not my wants. My cravings are just stupid gut feelings that make me feel as if I want to drink. But if I just think with my brain instead of my gut, my cravings will have to soon go away. And when they come back, I will just keep my mind on the fact that I honestly want to stop drinking, and they will have to go away again.

Every time I ignore my cravings they will become weaker and weaker. That's because, by ignoring them and refusing to take a drink, I will be training my body to stop craving altogether.

It won't be easy. Yes it will; all I will have to do is refuse to drink just one more time than I get a crave to drink. What could be easier than that? Nothing. As Dr. Maultsby said, it takes more energy to pick up a fifth of whiskey than it does to leave it sitting where it is; it may seem harder, but rational thinking makes me see that it's really easier; all I have to do is keep sincerely thinking: "I don't want a drink, I don't need a drink, and I definitely refuse to take a drink." Instead, I'll do something else: chew gum, jog, do push-ups, do sit-ups, read, drink coffee, or drink juice—anything that I like better than drinking. Then my stupid cravings will have to go away PDQ.

By this time Dr. Ryan would be six or seven minutes into listening to his voice recording. At least three times during that time, he will have already picked up, smelled, and put down a glass of his old favorite alcoholic drink and drunk several swallows from his glass of juice. He would also repeat that routine at least three more times while listening to the remainder of his nondrinking script which follows.

DR. RYAN'S SCRIPT CONTINUED

I used to think it was hard for me to refuse a drink. Now I see it is really easy. All I have to do is to say "NO" to my craving just one more time when it comes back. That's all, just one more time. Like now, my stupid craving is already almost gone. That guy on the tape was sure right about that.

Just by taking my mind off my craving, I can make it go away. So I have just proved to myself again how easy it is to refuse that first drink. All I have to do is think straight and concentrate on what I really want, instead of letting my stupid gut trick me into believing I want WHAT I REALLY DON'T WANT. It really boils down to rational mind over irrational gut.

The remainder of Dr. Ryan's script was almost the same as the latter part of our standard nondrinking script, so I won't repeat it here.

NO! But a few traditional alcohol counselors worry about that possibility. There are three reasons why their worry is irrational.

First, all the patients in our program come because they want to come.

Second, they can withdraw anytime they want to.

Third, while doing nondrinking practice, patients use only the ideas they have already convinced themselves they need to start acting out habitually.

None of those circumstances exists in brainwashing. Now let's see how one of the only legitimate experts on this technique of alcoholic self-help described it.

Dr. M.: Curly, now that you've had a few nondrinking sessions, tell me what they were like in the beginning, how you're experiencing them now, and whether or not you think they will be a help to you.

Curly: Well, the very first one was a real experience for me. Ah, I was, you know, like really uptight during most of the session. I walked into this little room. I really didn't know what to expect. Well, actually, they had told me what to expect, but I guess maybe I didn't believe them. But there was this little table there with a bottle of my favorite booze sitting, you know, right there as big as day. And I start to grab it and, you know, take a quick one. But then, well, you know, I caught myself and thought "Hey, wait a minute! What's happening here? What are these guys trying to pull?" All the other programs I'd been in, they tried to keep you away from booze, and here's a bottle sitting right here in front of me!! So, I sat down, you know, and thought "No! I better cool it." I wasn't sure what you all really wanted. But I still had this real strong craving. Then they came in and gave me this tape, and I listened to what the guy said. And, you know, like he really made some sense to me. And once I got into it, all of a sudden my craving was gone. And I said, "WOW!" You know, like I saw that I really could refuse to take that first drink.

Dr. M.: Sounds like it was a snap.

Curly: Well, not exactly. I mean, at first I couldn't hardly look at it, much less touch it; and at the end when you are supposed to pick it up and pour it out! HA, HA! Well, like, you know, I got sort of another little craving, and I thought maybe that I would take a little quick one. But then I thought, "I can't go out of here with alcohol on my breath." So I poured it out. And my craving went away just like magic; it was just like when I used to take antabuse and I would think "Sorry buddy, but like you know you can't drink today," and my cravings would disappear like magic.

Dr. M.: Okay, tell me about your later sessions.

Curly: Okay, like on the second day, the cravings were less and they went away faster. So, ah, I tried to do like the guy on the tape said; think about all the bad things, you know, that had happened; or, I should say, the bad things I had made happen when I was drinking. Then I thought about all the real good things that, uh, you know, could happen to me now, uh, that I've stopped drinking. So the second time it wasn't hard at all to pick it up and throw it down the drain.

I explained to Curly that some of what seemed to him to be a craving or urge to drink in his first practice session was really anxiety. He had habitually used alcohol largely to control his problem with free-floating anxiety. So anxiety about anything, as well as any other negative emotion, was a strong mental cue for him to take a drink. But as soon as he focused on that tape, the distraction of rational thinking about drinking quickly eliminated his cravings.

Curly's story clearly demonstrated the four self-help goals of nondrinking practice sessions:

First, **nondrinking practice sessions help problem drinkers extinguish their secondary alcoholic cravings.**

Second, **nondrinking practice sessions help problem drinkers stop being afraid to be around alcohol.** Instead, the problem drinkers begin to focus on the fact that a bottle of booze won't ever attack them first; therefore, they have no rational reason to attack it or even be afraid of it.

Third, **nondrinking practice sessions teach problem drinkers nondrinking thinking at the right time:** when they are face-to-face with a drink of their favorite booze.

Fourth, **nondrinking practice sessions teach problem drinkers to remember that the brain is much stronger than any secondary alcoholic cravings.**

EMPHASIS QUESTIONS

1. Problem drinkers don't understand the evils of alcohol. True or False?
2. The best time to give up drinking is after a drinking bout because you have a painful hangover. True or False?
3. Nondrinking practice is really brainwashing. True or False?
4. Some people want to write their own unique nondrinking script, and Dr. Maultsby encourages that practice. True or False?
5. The more _____ nondrinking thoughts _____ the personal _____ of problem drinkers, the _____.
6. Dr. Ryan was right; he was not exactly like the former problem drinker on the tape. True or False?

7. Because each problem drinker is unique, it's a waste of time to have standard nondrinking tape recordings and scripts. True or False?
8. Even though each problem drinker is _____ the alcoholic _____ process seems to be the _____ for all.
9. There are at least _____ reasons why nondrinking practice is not brainwashing.
10. List the three reasons from item 9.

   _____

   _____

   _____

CORRECT ANSWERS

1. False
2. False
3. False
4. True
5. accurately, describe, thoughts, better
6. True
7. False
8. unique, addictive, same
9. three
10. First, patients want to learn nondrinking thinking.
    Second, patients can stop nondrinking practice any time they want to.
    Third, before patients begin nondrinking practice sessions they have convinced themselves that it's best for them to do it.

17

Subtle Habits that Maintain Problem Drinking

ACTING OUT EMOTIONAL WHITE LIES

This means telling yourself an obvious lie, then reacting to your lie as if it were a fact. The following example of that irrational habit represents one of the main reasons problem drinkers refuse to benefit from treatment.

Dr. M.: Tell me, why did you refuse to benefit from any of the many alcoholic treatment programs you have been in?

Bob: The main reason was I was being forced to get treatment.

Dr. M.: Forced? How?

Bob: Yeah, well, like my wife would say, "You either go get treatment or I'm leaving." Or my parole officer would say he'd put me back in jail if I didn't go. So I'd go; but I wouldn't get involved.

Dr. M.: Oh, I see. In your mind you saw yourself as being forced into treatment.

Bob: And I wasn't going to let them get away with it.

Bob's Reaction Was Normal But Irrational

To see why, imagine this situation: Suppose you are comfortably seated in someone else's chair. You know it's someone else's chair and you have already decided to get up immediately when the person returns. But the person returns without your realizing he's back and says, "If you don't get out of my chair this second, I'll throw you out." What would be your natural tendency? To immediately jump up or to rebelliously SIT still?

Most people would have a strong urge to stubbornly sit tight; some others might even challenge the other person to make them get up, even though they initially had intended to get up without being asked. The point is, when people believe they are being forced to do something, even if they are inclined to do it, they tend to resist doing it.

Now let's relate that example to Bob's situation. Bob said, "I was being forced." The facts were his wife and parole officer would give him two choices, neither of which he wanted, but two choices just the same.

Bob didn't want to make either choice, but he would angrily choose the least undesirable one for him. Anger, however, is an inner urge to resist, even though there may not be any force to be resisted. That's why Bob felt as if he were being forced, even though he was making a choice.

Dr. M.: But you weren't being forced to get treatment; so it was inappropriate for you to be angry about going. No one was forcing you. They gave you two choices. Granted, you didn't want either one; but they were still choices, and you chose the one you believed was the least undesirable for you. But you still chose it. And because you did, it was unfair of you to blame your wife and parole officer for what you chose to do. All they did was say either you go for treatment or these undesirable things will happen.

Bob: (With a surprised look) You call that a choice?

Dr. M.: Of course that was a choice. It didn't seem like one to you because your gut reaction was the same intense anger you would have felt if they really had physically dragged you.

Bob: That's exactly how I felt: like I was being dragged against my will. That's why I was so PO'd.

Dr. M.: But did anyone physically overpower you and drag you to treatment?

Bob: Not physically.

Dr. M.: Well, if there is no physical contact, there can't be any objective force involved. That's an important insight, because Rational Self-Control is based on objective fact.

Bob: But what about my feeling? It actually felt like they were dragging me.

Dr. M.: And that's why you need to learn to think with your brain instead of your gut. The gut is a notorious Emotional White Liar.

Bob: (Puzzled) A what?

Dr. M.: Emotional White Liar. That means it makes you feel as if an obvious lie really is an obvious fact. People who do gut thinking instead of brain thinking often end up acting on emotional white lies, much to their own disadvantage, as well as that of others. I call them Rebels-Without-A-Cause.

All Rebels-Without-A-Cause have to do to make peace with themselves is repeat this obvious fact: "Regardless of how undesirable my choices were, I chose the one I chose; therefore, I have no rational reason to be angry or otherwise upset about it. And since I refuse to be a Rebel-Without-A-Cause, I'll calm myself down with the Instant Calming Maneuver (see chapter 11).

A subtle variation on the Rebel-Without-A-Cause syndrome causes the next excessive drinking habit.

PROVING THE OBVIOUS

One of the major signs of habitual problem drinking is increased tolerance for alcohol to at least twice that of social drinkers. Yet problem drinkers repeatedly drink themselves under the table, trying to prove the obvious: that they can drink and hold as much alcohol as any social drinker. But if those problem drinkers would only measure what they drink before they pass out, **they'd see that they can and regularly do hold two to four times as much alcohol as most social drinkers.**

The same mental blind spot that causes that excessive drinking habit also causes the next one.

CALLING THE EASIEST ACT THE HARDEST

Problem drinkers often say, "It's just too hard for me to stop drinking." Fortunately, they are mistaken. In fact, it takes more physical effort, and is therefore harder, to pick up a bottle than it does to refuse to pick it up. But before problem drinkers will refuse to pick up a bottle of booze, they must choose to refuse to do it. To make that choice, problem drinkers must get rid of the next excessive drinking habit.

HAVING THE RIGHT NONDRINKING IDEAS AT THE WRONG TIME

Problem drinkers are usually experts at accurately describing the evils and personal tragedies of problem drinking. But they habitually do it on the morning after when their bottles are empty. Nondrinking thinking then is a complete waste of time. What could be easier than refusing to drink when there is no drink to be drunk? The rational solution to problem drinking is habitually refusing to drink when full bottles of booze are just an arm's length away. Our nondrinking practice technique (Chapter 14) helps problem drinkers learn that rational habit. That highly effective technique is based on:

Four Important Facts

(1) People usually do what they are thinking about doing at the moment.

(2) People are most likely to think about doing a specific act at a specific time if they have already practiced thinking about doing it at that time.

(3) Practice means repeatedly thinking, emotionally feeling, and/or physically acting in one specific way.

(4) Nondrinking practice sessions give problem drinkers frequent practice in the right nondrinking thoughts, emotions, and physical actions at the best possible time—when a bottle of their favorite booze is sitting an arm's length away.

BEING AFRAID OF ALCOHOL

Alcoholics usually have long histories of fearlessly handling one bottle of alcohol after another. Yet when they dry out, they often become quite afraid of alcohol. If there is a bottle in their house, they often get so anxious and upset about it they end up drinking it as fast as possible, as a kind of self-defense. Their logic is: "It's dangerous for me to be around a bottle of booze. I'd better drink it up, so I won't have to worry about getting drunk." Then they get drunk.

When it's time for such problem drinkers to have their first nondrinking practice session, they fearfully ask, "Don't you think it's kind of risky to leave me by myself in a room with a bottle of my favorite poison?" "Not at all", we reassure them. Our bottles are tame. They won't ever attack you. Once you stop being afraid of alcohol, you will stop attacking it in self-defense.

EMPHASIS QUESTIONS

1. Briefly describe an example of telling an emotional white lie.
2. Briefly describe the irony of problem drinkers trying to prove they can hold their alcohol as well as social drinkers.
3. There really is a big difference between having no choices and having undesirable choices. True or False?
4. Resisting being forced to do things is a normal human _____.
5. When people admit to _____ to take personally undesirable actions, they are least likely to get _____ and _____ against taking them.
6. People often believe they were forced to take undesirable actions when in fact they chose to take those actions. True or False?
7. Mislabeling choice as force leads to being a _____-_____-_____-_____.
8. Problem drinkers often have the _____ idea about drinking, but at the _____ time.
9. Problem drinkers often call the _____ of two drinking tasks the more difficult.
10. Cured alcoholics sometimes drink as a kind of irrational _____-_____.

CORRECT ANSWERS

1. See page 209
2. See page 212
3. True
4. tendency
5. choosing, angry, rebel
6. True
7. Rebel-Without-A-Cause
8. right, wrong
9. easier
10. self-defense

18

Rational Self-Counseling to Prevent Alcohol Abuse

By
Paul Knipping, Ph.D.*

Our TV-addicted society is probably the best informed, yet most dissatisfied of any generation. The young and the old demonstrate their dissatisfaction with frequent illegal, immoral, antisocial, and self-destructive behavior. The powerful forces of modern social change are intensifying human adjustment problems by altering or cancelling the stabilizing effects of time-honored customs, such as marriage, religion, and traditional respect for authority. Human values are shifting and changing so rapidly that transience of commitment is the rule. In short, we are already in the ephemeral society described in *Future Shock*.

At the individual level, "future shock" usually means chronic emotional distress. Yet the TV illusion is that instant relief is not only possible, it's an inalienable right. Understandably, therefore, our society has turned in small part to illegal tranquilizing drugs and **almost completely to the legal ones.** Physicians write more than 150 million new prescriptions each year. Over half of them are for

---

*Dr. Knipping is an Associate Professor in Health Education at Texas Tech University, Lubbock, Texas.

tranquilizers. At the current new prescriptions rate, by the year 2000 every American adult and child could be on maintenance tranquilizers.

Compared to prescribed tranquilizers, alcohol is relatively cheap, fast, and reliable. Understandably, therefore, the alcoholic beverage industry is one of the largest and most profitable in our country.

So much for describing the obvious. What can society efficiently do to correct our unhealthy situation? As with most human problems, there are many different possible solutions. But I favor solutions that seem to have significant potential for being quick, economical and beneficial to the largest numbers of people at once. That's why I share Dr. Maultsby's enthusiasm for making "The Classroom an Emotional Health Center."

Almost everyone in our society goes to school. My research indicates that if our schools were to become appropriately involved, we could efficiently improve the emotional climate of our society.

Appropriate involvement of schools would mean schools teaching students the healthy use of their brains for creating rational self-concepts and developing skill in arriving at rational decisions, values, and goals.

Why the public schools? Why not let the mental health professionals take care of society's mental health needs? They just can't do it. There are not now enough mental health professionals to meet the needs of people who have **diagnosable** emotional illness. It is unrealistic, therefore, to expect these professionals to adequately meet the needs of the much larger school and nonschool population.

I recommend that we take our cue from the important insight Dr. Maultsby describes in his excellent book, *Help Yourself to Happiness*. "When people don't take drugs, their only emotional help is really self-help." That insight led me to the idea that Rational Self-Counseling, taught in schools, might be an ideal basis for effective yet practical community-based programs designed to prevent problem drinking, especially among adolescents.

Rational Self-Counseling and its research support have been adequately described in this and other books. All I will say is that my research data indicate RSC is useful as an aid to preventing emotional conflicts among university and public school (junior and senior high school) students. I am excited about that fact for two reasons.

First, Dr. Maultsby and many other mental health professionals have clearly shown that alcohol and other drug addictions are the accidental results of people trying to handle their emotional conflicts with those addictive drugs.

Second, school administrators in many areas conservatively estimate that at least 20 percent of junior and senior high school students are involved in abusive use of alcohol. Urban and central city school data reveal even higher levels of alcohol and other drug abuse.

Those two facts make it seem desirable to teach students short-term school-based emotional self-help programs that give lasting results. Rational Self-Counseling has all of those characteristics.

Failure of schools to provide education in emotional self-help seems analogous to:
- (a) stopping fluoridation and hiring more dentists.
- (b) omitting polio shots and manufacturing more prosthetic appliances.
- (c) distributing antibiotics to cholera patients and allowing them to drink from the same contaminated well.

The same logic applies to our national problems with alcohol abuse.

Rational Self-Counseling in the classroom as a strategy of emotional health intervention is no longer "experimental." Dr. Maultsby and I have repeatedly demonstrated the efficacy of RSC in a variety of school and school-like settings, including:
- (a) undergraduate classes at the University of Kentucky and Rockhurst College;
- (b) public and private schools in Lexington, Kentucky;
- (c) public schools (grade seven) in Farmington, Maine;
- (d) public schools (grade nine) in Lubbock, Texas;
- (e) classes made up of juvenile probation clients arrested for theft, drug abuse, and assault in Lubbock, Texas.

At the University of Kentucky subjects were recruited from upperclassmen enrolled in health education classes. Eighty students were divided into two groups of forty; both groups had comparable

---

*These inventories were Shostrom's Personal Orientation Inventory and Rotter I-E.

backgrounds and educational abilities. Both groups were given two personality tests* to estimate their current emotional health. One group was then designated our "control" group and therefore received no self-help instruction. But our "experimental" group was taught RSC.

Our experimental group attended sixteen sessions, each two and a half hours long, one afternoon per week. The course format was:

(a) Indirect exposure to the teacher-counselor (Dr. Maultsby) by viewing videotapes. These tapes demonstrated rational self-counseling sessions conducted by Dr. Maultsby with people who had emotional problems typical of college students.

(b) Each week students were assigned self-help reading in Dr. Maultsby's book: *Help Yourself to Happiness,* and were required to do detailed written rational self-analysis of personal problems. Those who did not have personal problems they wanted to work on in class were assigned AS-IF problems and RSA's from Dr. Maultsby's self-help book entitled *"You and Your Emotions."*

(c) During the last half of the semester the class met in groups of ten for group discussions of their analyzed problems. Each student, in alphabetical order, was appointed group leader for one session.

CONCLUSIONS

Our study indicated that RSC taught in the classroom **does** enable students to improve their emotional health. At the end of sixteen weeks, both groups of students were given the same personality tests. The group who had been taught RSC had significantly improved scores on their personality tests; but those students who did not receive self-help instructions showed no significant change.*

In public and private schools (Lexington, Kentucky) similar studies were conducted using 2" X 2" transparencies. Unlike videotapes or film strips, transparencies can be re-edited, reordered, omitted, or added with ease. Transparencies (color or black and

---

*Significant positive change was $p < .05$ on statistical analysis.

white) enabled us to easily tailor the class material to the needs of the student groups. In addition, students were shown videotaped materials and were required to do written rational self-analyses.

CONCLUSION

These studies indicated that, given **appropriate teaching materials,** regular classroom teachers can have a positive influence on students' emotional control.

Public schools in Farmington, Maine served as additional testing grounds for RSC's effects. Twelve classes of seventh graders were chosen in four different schools. In two of the schools the experimental classes were given only traditional information on alcohol abuse. These included pamphlets **(What Everyone Should Know About Alcohol and Guide for the Family of the Alcoholic)** and films (including **The Summer We Moved To Elm Street and Boozers and Users).**

The other two experimental classes were given only information on Rational Self-Counseling. This material included transparencies, videotapes, and written handouts, all "home-crafted" and relatively inexpensive.

In each school two classes were experimental, while a third comparable class acted as a control and did not receive any alcohol abuse materials or RSC materials.

All the classes took tests before the introduction of any materials into the classroom. These tests were Shostrom's Personality Orientation Inventory and an alcohol inventory developed at Teacher's College, Columbia University. After the experiment the same tests were given to all classes and the following changes in test scores were noted.

In the Rational Self-Counseling study the control group showed some gain in nine categories but only one was significant at the $p < .05$ level. Control groups often show such small improvements as a result of becoming more familiar with the tests the second time, or because between testing they have fortuitously learned something that improved their test score.

The experimental (Rational Self-Counseling) groups showed

gains in eleven categories, and nine of these were significant at the $p < .05$ level of confidence.

In the group using the traditional alcohol abuse material the control group again showed positive improvement, this time in fourteen categories, five of which were significant. The experimental groups also showed positive improvement in fourteen categories, and twelve of those positive changes were at the $p < .05$ level of confidence.

CONCLUSIONS

These data afford some interesting observations. First, just giving the tests, particularly the alcohol inventory tests, may raise slightly the students' consciousness of alcohol abuse as well as teach them helpful information about alcohol.

Second, for teaching seventh graders about alcohol abuse, presenting them standard information about the results of alcohol abuse is somewhat more effective than merely teaching Rational Self-Counseling using makeshift, alcohol-related graphic aids.

Third, Rational Self-Counseling is more effective than doing nothing to teach seventh graders about alcohol abuse. That may mean that teaching seventh graders how to think rationally makes them less susceptible to environmental inducements for alcohol abuse. Furthermore, the effectiveness of the makeshift graphic aids used in Rational Self-Counseling compared favorably with that of the professionally prepared alcohol abuse materials. These facts demonstrate that Rational Self-Counseling has potential for low-cost self-help programs.

Because of the similarity of results produced by those two distinctly different approaches, more studies are being done of the long term effect of including Rational Self-Counseling in the classroom approach to preventing alcohol abuse among junior and senior high school students.

An early study done in Lubbock, Texas with ninth grade students indicated that Rational Self-Counseling had a strong positive effect in teaching students appropriate attitudes about alcohol abuse.

Another group of teenagers in legal trouble in Lubbock, Texas revealed even more dramatic evidence that teaching Rational Self-

Counseling can produce significant positive changes in attitudes. Juvenile probation authorities in Lubbock introduced us to a group of fifteen male teenagers who had been arrested for one or more of the following: drug related charges, assaults, and theft. These were all first offenders who were given the choice of appearing in court to receive appropriate sentences—or attending ten two-hour sessions on Rational Self-Counseling.

Studies by workers in many fields of psychology and sociology have produced very little evidence than any treatment significantly influences the outcome behavior of such male juveniles on probation. It is noteworthy therefore that our post-Rational Self-Counseling tests showed significant positive change in the anticipated direction of improvements in self-image, self-regard, and acceptance of authority. Improvement in those three areas of personality development is usually a precursor of behavioral improvement.

Theft, drug abuse, and assault all have predisposing judgmental and emotional components. Rational Self-Counseling may well provide young offenders less susceptibility to irrational judgments and emotions, which lead them into legal difficulty. I say that because after seven months of follow-up on these teenagers, none of the fifteen had become second offenders. The replication of this study with longer term follow-up provisions is being planned.

CONCLUSIONS

Those data indicate that with appropriate teaching materials, Rational Self-Counseling produces positive attitudinal changes in public school students. As an aid to self-rehabilitation Rational Self-Counseling may prove to be the most cost effective approach for probated juveniles, inside as well as outside the regular school system.*

---

*Michael Ruhnow of the Federal Probations Office, Dallas, Texas is doing research that supports that expectation.

SUMMARY

Available experimental data suggest that teaching Rational Self-Counseling is appropriate for use in public school classrooms.

The evidence also indicates that classroom RSC can produce:

(a) rational decisions among junior and senior high school students about alcohol and other drug abuse, as well as other deviant behaviors;

(b) rational value-clarifying activities;

(c) improved interaction with other individuals.

I'd like to emphasize that the degree of success with Rational Self-Counseling depends primarily on the intensity of its application. The goal is to overcome habitual, self-defeating attitudes and beliefs. As with all habits, these cognitive habits tend to persist unless the individual challenges them **rationally, relentlessly** and **repeatedly.** That's why the regular classroom approach for mental, emotional and behavioral re-education is ideal. The persistent, consistently re-inforced, structured learning format of schools is much more ideal for efficient, economical, behavioral change in moderately distressed adolescents than are the expensive, inefficient traditional mental and emotional health maneuvers.

YIPE TEST

Name_____

Age_____   Date mo._____, day____, yr._____

    This form describes common perceptions, beliefs and reactions almost all people have. By completing it fully and honestly you will help us quickly understand the unique person you are. Please read each item carefully and circle the response that best describes you MOST OF THE TIME.

Definitions

(1) NEVER means less than 10% of the time
(2) SOMETIMES means about 25% of the time
(3) AS OFTEN AS NOT means about 50% of the time
(4) FREQUENTLY means about 75% of the time
(5) USUALLY means more than 90% of the time.

		Never	Sometimes	As Often As Not	Frequently	Usually
1.	I believe I need more self-confidence.	(1)	(2)	(3)	(4)	(5)
2.	I believe I am a born worrier.	(1)	(2)	(3)	(4)	(5)
3.	I believe I act differently than I feel.	(1)	(2)	(3)	(4)	(5)
4.	No one seems to care enough about me.	(1)	(2)	(3)	(4)	(5)
5.	I believe that many of my emotional problems would be solved if people would just be honest with me.	(1)	(2)	(3)	(4)	(5)
6.	I am dissatisfied with myself as a person	(1)	(2)	(3)	(4)	(5)
7.	I feel hurt if people mistreat me.	(1)	(2)	(3)	(4)	(5)

	Never	Sometimes	As Often As Not	Frequently	Usually
8. I feel anxious, or nervous, or "high-strung" almost like I am waiting for some unknown, terrible thing to happen.	(1)	(2)	(3)	(4)	(5)
9. I actually hate myself	(1)	(2)	(3)	(4)	(5)
10. I get upset about trivial things.	(1)	(2)	(3)	(4)	(5)
11. I wake up feeling afraid to face the day	(1)	(2)	(3)	(4)	(5)
12. I don't like being left alone for many hours or a day at a time.	(1)	(2)	(3)	(4)	(5)
13. There are past events I still get angry or depressed over.	(1)	(2)	(3)	(4)	(5)
14. What some other people think of me is as important to me as what I think of myself.	(1)	(2)	(3)	(4)	(5)
15. I feel like two different people at the same time.	(1)	(2)	(3)	(4)	(5)
16. I feel guilty about my failures.	(1)	(2)	(3)	(4)	(5)
17. When I am upset or angry about something or someone, I am likely to say things like "Why does everything have to happen to me?" or "How could he or she have done such a thing?"	(1)	(2)	(3)	(4)	(5)
18. In order to get people to like me, I act the way I think they want me to.	(1)	(2)	(3)	(4)	(5)
19. My emotions change from one extreme to another within minutes without me knowing why.	(1)	(2)	(3)	(4)	(5)

		Never	Sometimes	As Often As Not	Frequently	Usually
20.	I give up quickly when attempting a difficult task, then I feel dissatisfied with myself.	(1)	(2)	(3)	(4)	(5)
21.	I feel lonely and uncomfortable.	(1)	(2)	(3)	(4)	(5)
22.	I feel inferior to some other people.	(1)	(2)	(3)	(4)	(5)
23.	It upsets me that I have trouble making decisions.	(1)	(2)	(3)	(4)	(5)
24	I feel depressed.	(1)	(2)	(3)	(4)	(5)
25	It upsets me that I have problems getting along with people.	(1)	(2)	(3)	(4)	(5)
26	I find myself thinking about things I don't want to think about.	(1)	(2)	(3)	(4)	(5)
27.	I worry so much about what others think of me, that I find myself not doing the things I want to do.	(1)	(2)	(3)	(4)	(5)
28.	When faced with a difficult task or something that I don't want to do, I am likely to start thinking that "I can't do it."	(1)	(2)	(3)	(4)	(5)
29.	I feel badly knowing that someone doesn't care for me as much as I care for them.	(1)	(2)	(3)	(4)	(5)
30.	I don't get over emotional hurt quickly.	(1)	(2)	(3)	(4)	(5)
31.	I really get upset if I think that I have been used.	(1)	(2)	(3)	(4)	(5)
32.	I really get upset if I think people are thinking bad things about me.	(1)	(2)	(3)	(4)	(5)
33.	I feel that I am worthless.	(1)	(2)	(3)	(4)	(5)

		Never	Sometimes	As Often As Not	Frequently	Usually
34.	My feelings are hurt easily.	(1)	(2)	(3)	(4)	(5)
35.	If I don't stay a little tense about things I have to do, I forget to do them.	(1)	(2)	(3)	(4)	(5)
36.	I refuse to accept myself when I fail.	(1)	(2)	(3)	(4)	(5)
37.	I don't seem to be as good a person as I can and ought to be.	(1)	(2)	(3)	(4)	(5)
38.	My life seems worthless and unproductive.	(1)	(2)	(3)	(4)	(5)
39.	It seems to me that I am a failure.	(1)	(2)	(3)	(4)	(5)
40.	It seems to me that I don't live up to my potential (abilities and talents).	(1)	(2)	(3)	(4)	(5)
41.	When things that really matter to me don't go right, it upsets me very much.	(1)	(2)	(3)	(4)	(5)
42.	If certain people cared enough for me, my problems would be solved.	(1)	(2)	(3)	(4)	(5)
43.	I have tried to change myself, but it seems I can't do it.	(1)	(2)	(3)	(4)	(5)
44.	When I decide to be carefree and loose, something bad seems to happen.	(1)	(2)	(3)	(4)	(5)
45.	It seems to me that I am not intelligent enough.	(1)	(2)	(3)	(4)	(5)

(The End)

REFERENCES

The particular book sections or chapters for which each of the below-listed publications is relevant are indicated in parentheses in bold type at the end of each listing.

Armor, D.J., et al. Alcoholism and Treatment. New York: John Wiley & Son, 1978. **(15)**

Beritoff, J.S., Neutral Mechanisms of Higher Vertebrate Behavior (Translated by W.T. Liberson) Boston: Little, Brown & Co., 1965. **(1,4,5,6,8,9,13,14,15,16,17)**

Brandsma, J., Maultsby, M.C. and Welsh, R. Self-Help Techniques in the Treatment of Alcoholism: Terminal Report. N.I.A.A.A. Grant # 2ROI AA-406-05, 1978. **(Introduction)**

Eccles, J.C., "The Physiology of Imagination," Scientific American, Sept., 1958, Vol. 199, p. 135. **(8,9,11,13,14,15,16,17)**

Ellis, Albert, Reason and Emotion in Psychotherapy, New York: Lyle Stuart, 1963. **(Professional Acknowledgement)**

Ellis, A., "Rational Emotive Therapy," Ch. 10 in Operational Theories of Personality, Edited by Burton, A., New York: Brunner-Mazel, 1974, p. 308-344. **(Professional Acknowledgement)**

Epictetus, Discourses of Epictetus (translated by George Long) London: George Bell & Sons, 1888. **(3,4,5,6)**

Gibbins, R.J. et al. Research Advances in Alcohol and Drug Problems, Vol. 2, New York: John Wiley & Son, 1975. **(Introduction)**

Grace, W.J., and Graham, D.T., "Relationship of Specific Attitudes and Emotions to Certain Bodily Disease," Psychosom. Med., 1952, 14: 243-251. **(4,5,6,13,17)**

Graham, D.T., "Some Research on Psychophysiologic Specificity and its Relation to Psychosomatic Disease", in R. Roessler and N.S. Greenfield (Eds.); Physiological Correlates of Psychological Disorder, Madison: University of Wisconsin Press, 1962. **(4,5,6,13,17)**

Graham, D.T., Kabler, J.D., and Graham, F.K., "Physiological Response to the Suggestion of Attitudes Specific for Hives and Hypertension", Psychosom. Med., 1962, 24:159-169. **(4,5,6,13,17)**

Graham, D.T., Lundy, R.M., Benjamin, L.S., Kabler, J.D., Lewis, W.C., Kunish, N.Q., and Graham, F.K., "Specific Attitudes in Initial Interviews with Patients Having Different Psychosomatic Diseases," Psychosom. Med., 1962, 24:257-266. **(4,5,6,13,17)**

Graham, D.T., Stern, J.A., and Winokur, G., "The Concept of a Different Specific Set of Physiological Changes in Each Emotion," Psychiatric Research Reports, 12, American Psychiatric Association, Jan. 1960. **(4,5,6,13,17)**

Graham, D.T., Stern, J.A., and Winokur, G., "Experimental Investigation of the

Specificity of Attitude Hypothesis in Psychosomatic Disease," <u>Psychosom. Med.,</u> 1958, 20:446-457. **(4,5,6,13,17)**

Hebb, D.O., The Organization of Behavior, New York: John Wiley & Sons, Inc., 1959. **(1,4,5)**

Holland, J.G., and Skinner, B.F., The Analysis of Behavior, New York: McGraw-Hill, 1961. **(1,4,5,6,8,9,14,15,16,17)**

Hudgins, C.V., "Conditioning and Voluntary Control Reflex," <u>J. Gen. Psych.,</u> 1933, 8:1-49. **(1,4,5,6,11,14,15,16)**

Jones, K. et al. Attribution: Perceiving the Causes of Behavior, Morristown, NJ: General Learning Press, 1971. **(1,4,5,6,8,9,13,14,15,16,17)**

Knipping, P. and Chadler, L.B. "A Classroom Comparison of Behavioral Modification Techniques." <u>The Journal of School Health,</u> XLV, no. 1, (Jan. 1975), 33-36. **(18)**

Knipping, P., Maultsby, M.C., and Thompson, P. "The Technology for Using the Classroom as an Emotional Health Center." <u>The Journal of School Health,</u> XLVI, **(18)**

Knipping, P., Maultsby, M.C. "Rational Self-Counseling, Primary Prevention to Alcohol Abuse." <u>Journal of Alcohol and World Health Research,</u> 2,1 (Fall, 1977), 31-35. **(18)**

Ludwig, Arnold, M. "Craving and Relapse to Drink," <u>Quarterly Journal of Studies on Alcohol,</u> March, 1974, Vol. 35, No. 1, pp. 899-905. **(2,6,9,14,16)**

Ludwig, Arnold, M., Wikler, A., "The First Drink," <u>Archives of General Psychiatry,</u> April, 1974, Vol. 30, pp. 539-547. **(2,6,9,14,16)**

Luria, A.R., The Working Brain (translated by Haigh) New York: Basic Books, 1973. **(1,4,5,6,8,9,10,11,13,14,16,17)**

MacLean, P.D., "Chemical and Electrical Stimulation of Hippocampus in Unrestrained Animals: II Behavioral Findings," <u>Arch. Neurol. & Psychiat.,</u> 1957, 78:128. **(1,3,4)**

MacLean, P.D., "Contrasting Functions of Limbic and Neocortical Systems of the Brain and Their Relevance to Psychophysiological Aspects of Medicine," <u>Am. J. Med.,</u> 1958, 25:611. **(1,3,4)**

Maultsby, M.C., "Rational Emotive Imagery," <u>Rational Living,</u> 1971, 6(1), 24-26. **(2,6,11,14,16,17)**

Maultsby, M.C., "The Relapse Patient in RBT," Growth Through Reason. Palo Alto, Calif.: Science and Behavior Book Co., 1971. **(1,2,3,6,17)**

Maultsby, M.C., "Routine Tape Recorder Use in RET," <u>Rational Living,</u> 1970, 5(1), 8-23. **(2,3,16)**

Maultsby, M.C., "Systematic Written Homework in Psychotherapy," <u>Psychotherapy: Theory Research and Practice,</u> 1971 8(3), 195-198. **(2,3,7,10,12,18)**

Maultsby, M.C., "Written Homework for the Patient with an Emotional Crisis," <u>American Family Physician,</u> 1971. **(2,3,7,10,12)**

Maultsby, M.C., and Graham, D.T., "Controlled Study of Effects of Psychotherapy on Self-Reported Maladaptive Traits, Anxiety Scores, and Psychosomatic Disease Attitudes," J. of Psychoa. Res., 1974, Vol. 10:121-132. (1,3,6,7,13,17)

Maultsby, M.C., and Gram, Joyce, "A Two Year Follow-up Study of Rational Behavior Therapy," Paper presented at the 5th Annual Meeting of the Behavioral Therapists in Washington, D.C., September 6, 1971. (2,3)

Maultsby, M.C., and Gram, J.M., "Patients' Responses to the Use of Tape Recorders in Psychotherapy: A Clinical Study of 56 Patients," J. of Nat'l. Med. Assoc., 1972, 64(4):375. (2,3,16)

Maultsby, M.C., Help Yourself to Happiness Through Rational Self-Counseling. New York Institute for Rational Living, 1976. (2,3,4,5,6,7,8,9,10,11,12, 13,14,15,16,17,18)

Maultsby, M.C., "Evolution of Rational Behavior Therapy," Proceeding of The Annual Conference of Rational Emotive and Behavioral Therapist. Chicago, Illinois, 1975. (Professional Acknowledgement, 4,5,6,10,11)

Maultsby, M.C., Knipping, P., and Carpenter, L. "Teaching Self-Help in the Classroom with Rational Self-Counseling." The Journal of School Health, XLIV, no. 8 (October, 1974), 445-448. (18)

Maultsby, M.C. and Stiefel, L., "A Theory of Rational Behavioral Group Process," Rational Living, 1972, 7(1):28-34. (3,15)

Maultsby, M.C., and Winkler, P.J., "Directed Rational Self-Counseling (A New Approach to Mass Mental Health)," 1972 ANA Clinical Sessions. (2,3,7)

Mowrer, O.H., Learning Theory and Behavior, New York: John Wiley & Sons, 1960. (1,4,5,17)

Mowrer, O.H., Learning Theory and the Symbolic Process, New York: John Wiley & Sons, 1963. (1,4,5,6,9,14,15,17)

Nietzel, M.T., et al., Behavioral Approaches to Community Psychology. New York: Pergamon Press, 1977. (Introduction, 15)

O'Leary, K.D. and Wilson, G., Behavior Therapy, Englewood Cliffs, NJ: Prentice-Hall, 1975. (Introduction)

Patterson, E.M., et al., Emerging Concepts of Alcohol Dependence, New York: Springer, 1977. (Introduction, 1)

Pelletier, Kenneth R., Mind As Healer Mind as Slayer. New York: Dell Publishing Co., 1977. (18)

Piaget, J., The Judgement and Reason in the Child, New York: Harcourt, Brace & World, 1929. (4,5,6)

Piaget, J., Logic and Psychology, New York: Basic Books, 1957. (4,5,6)

Razran, G., "The Observable Unconscious and the Inferable Conscious in Current Soviet Psychophysiology: Interoceptive Conditioning, Semantic Conditioning and the Orienting Reflex," Psych. Rev., 1961, 68:81-147. (1,4,5,6,9,13,14,15,16,17)

Razran, G., Attitudinal determines of conditioning and generalization of conditioning, Journal of Experimental Psychology, 1949, 39, 820-829. (1,3,4,5,6,7,8,9,13,14,15,16,17)

Razran, G., Conditioned response: An experimental study and a theoretical analysis, Archives of Psychology, 1935, 28, (Whole No. 191), (1,3,4,5,6,7,8,9,13,14,15,16,17)

Rokeach, Milton, The Open and Closed Mind, New York: Basic Books, 1960. (1,2,4,5,6,8,9)

Rotter, J.B., Psychological Monographs. 80 Whole No. 609, 1966. (1,2,4,5,6,8,9)

Rotter, J.B., Social Learning and Clinical Psychology, New York: Prentice Hall, Inc., 1954. (4,5,6,14,15,16,17)

Russell, P.L. and Brandsma, J.M., A theoretical and empirical integration of the rational emotive and classical conditioning theories, Journal of Consulting and Clinical Psychology, 1974, 42, 189-197. (1,4,5,6,11,14,15,16,17)

Schachter, S., "The Interaction of Cognitive and Physiologic Determinants of Emotional States," Ad. Exp. Soc. Psych., 1964, 1:49-80. (1,4,5,6,7,8,9,16,17)

Skinner, B.F., The Behavior of Organisms, New York: Appleton-Century, 1938. (1,4,5,6,14,15,16,17)

Skinner, B.F., Science and Human Behavior, New York: The Free Press, 1960. (1,4,5,6,14,15,16,17)

Skinner, B.F., Verbal Behavior, New York: Appleton-Century-Crofts, 1957. (4,5,6,8,9,14,15,16,17)

Solnitzky, O., "The Limbic System: Its Relation to Personality," Georgetown Med. Bull., 1964, 17:161. (4,5)

Staats, A.W. and Staats, C.K., Attitudes established by classical conditioning, Journal of Abnormal and Social Psychology, 1958, 57, 37-40. (1,3,4,5,6,7,8,9,13,14,15,16,17)

Staats, A.W. and Staats, C.K., Language conditioning of meaning to meaning using a semantic generalization paradigm, Journal of Experimental Psychology, 1959, 57, 187-192. (1,3,4,5,6,7,8,9,13,14,15,16,17)

Staats, A.W. and Staats, C.K., Meaning established by classical conditioning, Journal of Experimental Psychology, 1957, 54, 74-80. (1,4,5,6,8,9,13,14,15,16,17)

Toffler, Alvin, Future Shock, New York: Random House, 1970. (18)

Tolman, E.C., "Cognitive Maps in Rats and Men," Psychol. Rev., 1948, 53:189. (4,5,6,14,15,16,17)

Ullman, L.P. and Krasner, L., A Psychological Approach To Abnormal Behavior, (2nd. ed.) Englewood Cliffs, NJ: Prentice-Hall, 1975. (**Introduction**)

Watson, J.B. and Rayner, R., Conditioned emotional reactions, Journal of Experimental Psychology, 1920, 3, 1-14. (1,4,5,6,11,14,15,16,17)

Wikler, A. "Requirements for Extinction of Relapse-Facilitating Variables and for Rehabilitation in a Narcotic-Antagonist Treatment Program," Advances in Biochemical Psychopharmacology, 1974, Vol. 8, p. 399-414. (2,6,9,14,15,16)

Wikler, A. "Some Implications of Conditioning Theory for Problems of Drug

Abuse," Behavioral Science, January, 1971, Vol. 16, p. 92-97. **(2,6,9, 14,15,16)**

Wikler, A., and Pescor, Frank T., "Persistence of 'Relapse - Tendencies' of Rats Previously Made Physically Dependent on Morphine," Psychopharmacologia, 1970, 16, 375-384. **(2,6,9,14,15,16)**

Wikler, A., Theories related to physical dependence, The Chemical and Biological Aspects of Drug Dependence, Cleveland: Chemical Rubber Company Press, 1972. **(2,6,8,9,14,15,16)**

Wikler, A., Dynamics of drug dependence: Implications of a conditioning theory for research and treatment. Archives of General Psychiatry, 1973, 28, 611-616. **(2,6,8,9,14,15,16)**

INDEX

A

AA, 4, 5, 6
ABC's, emotional, 50, 53, 55, 58, 61, 62, 63, 64, 73, 80, 186
"ABC's of Alcoholic Self-Help," 68, 70, 72
"ABC's of Rational Self-Analysis," 120
abstinence, 37, 194
activating event, see RSA
addiction, 11, 30, 97, 98, 105, 111, 202, 218; see also smoking
adolescent drinking, 23ff
alcoholics, number of, 1
Alcoholics Anonymous, 4, 5, 6
alcoholism, see also Habitual Problem Drinking
    accidental, 30, 217
    cost of, 1
    compulsive drinking, 30, 32
    cues for drinking, 109, 119, 179, 192, 207
    denial of drinking, 17, 18, 38, 202
mental dependence, 29, 33, 40, 109, 112, 119
    motivation, 2, 10, 24, 25; see also problems
    obsession with drinking, 29, 32, 39
    physical dependence, 30, 31, 33, 119, 202
    stage one, 29, 119, 202
    stage two, 29, 30, 32, 97, 202
"always," 184
anemia, 2
anger, 15ff, 25, 94, 99, 126, 127, 149, 153, 161, 165, 166, 199, 209ff
antabuse, 38, 97, 206
anxiety, 207
as-if RSA, 154
attitudes, 46, 47, 64, 65, 68, 72, 73, 95, 102, 175; in RSA, 124, 152, 158; see also ABCs

B

behavior, see cognitive, emotive, physical
behavioral re-education, 173, 178, 182, 186
beliefs, 46, 47, 64, 68, 72, 73, 83, 95, 102, 115; in RSA, 123, 158, 161, 175; see also perceptions; see also RSA; see also ABCs
black-outs, 29
Bob's case history, 23ff, 33ff, 74ff, 108ff, 149ff, 216ff
bored, 199
brain, 21, 36, 44, 46, 54, 71, 112, 118, 138, 163
brainwashing, 204ff

Brandsma, Dr. Jeffrey, 5
Bureau of Health Resources, 6

C

calm, see emotions, neutral; see instant maneuver; see RSA
camera, see brain
camera check, see RSA
Carpenter, Linda, 7
case histories
    Bob (adolescence), 23ff
    Bob (smoking), 108ff
    Bob (emotional satisfaction), 34, 37, 74ff
    Bob (fear of withdrawal), 33ff
    Bob (first RSA, for anger), 149ff
    Green (lonliness), 13ff, 37, 124, 131ff
    Ryan (anger, stress), 17ff, 37ff, 201ff
catch-22, 2
cigarettes, see smoking
classrooms, 217ff
cognitive behavior and/or habits, 44, 45, 46, 72, 182, 184
cognitive-emotive dissonance, see dissonance
cold turkey, see withdrawal
compulsive drinking, 30, 32
conflict, 87, 183; see also rational, rules of
consequences, see RSA
counselors, 6, 154, 167, 177, 183, 188, 205, 218; see also psychotherapists; see also RBT; see also RSC
craving, see primary alcoholic craving; see secondary alcoholic craving
"craving" versus "wanting," 97, 115, 116, 202, 203
crime, 34ff, 74ff, 216, 218, 221
cues for drinking, 109, 119, 179, 192, 207; see also smoking
cures for drinking, 99, 103, 105, 106, 109, 178, 209ff (resisting cures); see also New Self Help Alcoholic Treatment; see also Intensive Self-Help

D

daily home-life plan, see home-life plan
de-addiction, 115; see also addiction
debate, see RSA
delirium tremens, 32ff, 99, 100
denial of alcoholism, 17, 18, 38
depression, 25, 34, 99, 105, 199
detoxification, see withdrawal
diarrhea, 174
dissonance, 173-177

drinking, see habitual problem drinking; see alcoholism
driver re-education, 175ff
drugs, see addiction
"dry DTs," 99, 100
"drying out," see withdrawal
DTs, 32ff, 99, 100

E

early problem drinkers, 27; see also social drinking
educators, 7, 13ff, 220
Ellis, Dr. Albert, see acknowledgement
embarrassment, 127
emotional ABC's, see ABC's
Emotional White Liar, 211
emotions; see also ABC's
    lack of, 130, 131
    negative, 55, 71, 82, 89
    neutral, 58
    positive, 53
    what they do, 80
emotive behavior or habits, 44, 45, 72, 80, 103, 182; see also REI for learning new emotional habits
emphasis questions, 8-9, 25-26, 41-42, 48-49, 60, 68-69, 78-79, 95-96, 106-107, 120-21, 135-37, 145-46, 155-56, 169-70, 180-81, 207-08, 215
evaluative thoughts, 52, 54, 70, 72, 96

F

"fact" versus "truth," 11, 21, 84
Fallible Human Being, 128
"falling off the wagon," see relapse
family of alcoholics, 5, 29, 39, 183, 209, 220; see also case history, Mrs. Green
fear, 66, 67, 95, 185; see also motivation; see also case history, Bob, for fear of withdrawal
fear of alcohol, 214
FHB, see Fallible Human Being
first drink, 172, 177, 178, 198ff, 204, 206
follow-up care, 193
Future Shock, 216

G

Gaffield, Susan, 7
gastritis, 2
GO signs for drinking, 28, 194

goals, see RSA
"got to have", see "need"
Green, Mrs., case history, 13ff, 37, 124, 131ff
Greene, Dr. Mary, 8
guilt, 25
gut-feeling, see gut-thinking
gut-thinking, 72, 73, 74, 75, 95, 96

H

habits, 28, 62, 138, 139, 172, 175; see also behavioral re-education; see also cognitive habits; see also emotive habits; see also physical habits
habitual problem drinking, 1, 3, 6, 12, 16, 25, 27, 29, 33, 36, 47ff, 68, 99, 172
Help Yourself to Happiness, 217, 218
home-life plan, 192
homeostasis, 30, 174, 202
hopes and desires, 101, 102, 103; see also motivation

I

ICM, 140
inhibitions, removal of, 19, 34, 74, 75
Insight, Emotional, 52, 54
Insight, Rational, 84, 85, 89
Insight psychotherapy, 5, 6
Instant Calming Maneuver, 140, 212
"instant relief", 216
Intensive Self-Help Alcoholic Treatment Program, 7, 8, 29, 37, 163, 169, 182ff, 194
interruptions in problem drinking, 177
Irrational Self-Counseling, 45
irrational, see rational
irrational "should's", see should's
"IT", 50, 58, 59, 159

J

jumping off the wagon, see relapse

K

Knipping, Dr. P., 216, 223

L

learned urges, 105
liver damage, 2
loneliness, 14ff

M

malnutrition, 2
martyrs, 105
medical treatment, 1, 2, 97, 98
mental dependence on alcohol, 29, 33, 40, 109, 112, 119
mental images, 21
motivation, 2, 10, 24, 25

N

nagging, 15, 16
"needing" a drink, 100, 102, 115, 125, 134, 198; see also "wanting" a drink; see also hope and desire; see also "craving" versus "needing"
needs, objective, 102; subjective, 102; see also needing
negative reinforcement, 29
nervousness, 25
"never," 184
New Self Help Alcoholic Treatment Method, 4, 6, 12, 13, 178, 194, 196
"no emotions," 130, 131, 184
nondrinking practice, 178ff, 196, 198, 201, 207, 213, 214
nondrinking script, see script
nonlearned urges, 105
nosey neighbors, 149ff
"now", 166, 216

O

obsession with drinking, 29, 30, 38

P

Pavlov, 116
perceptions, 53, 103, 184; see also ABC's
personal problems, see problems and alcohol; see 183ff for problems dealt with in intensive program; see also individual names of problems, such as fear, loneliness, depression
personality testing, 182, 218, 219
physical behavior or habits, 44, 45, 72, 80, 182
physical dependence on alcohol, 30, 31, 33, 119; see also addiction
physicians, 6, 17ff, 33, 36, 43, 154, 165, 216
pneumonia, 2
practicing mentally, 63, 110, 116-18, 138-45, 173, 177, 178, 187, 197, 213; see also REI
prescriptions, 216
primary alcoholic craving, 31, 97, 99, 100, 103, 105, 109, 113, 116
problem drinking, see habitual problem drinking
problems and alcohol, 3, 5, 10, 11, 12, 27, 29; see also individual names of problems such as fear, loneliness, depression

psychotherapy, practice, 4, 5, 36, 43, 217; research, 5, 6; RBT training, 6, 48, 81; see also RSA, especially 147, 167

Q

questions, see emphasis questions; see rational questions

R

Rand Report, 194
Rational Emotive Imagery, 5, 47, 138-45, 173, 201
Rational Behavior Therapy, 5, 6, 68, 105, 134, 154, 193
rational, rules for, 44-45, 82, 83, 85, 86, 87, 88
rational, questions for, 90 ff. 123, 150, 158
Rational Self-Analysis
   as-if, 154
   directions, 120, 122, 186, 189
   format, 120
      activating event, 123
      beliefs, 124
      consequences, 125
      five questions, 125
      camera check, 126
      rational debate of beliefs, 127
      expected new behavior, 129
      telephone, 193
Rational Self-Counseling
   appropriate patients, 41, 163, 217ff
   definition, 44, 83
   problem-solving, 184, 187
   re-education, 175
   research, 4, 5, 217ff
   schools, 7
   self-disclosure in RSC, 113
   tape recordings in RSC, 110
rattlesnake, 67
"rebel without a cause" syndrome, 22, 211, 212
refusing that first drink, 172, 173
REI, see Rational Emotive Imagery
rejection, fear of, 24
relapse, 1, 97, 98, 99, 100, 115, 120, 173, 178, 193
repetition, 62, 110, 172, 173
research, 4, 5, 28, 47, 48, 52, 67, 111, 139, 169, 175, 194, 217
revolutionaries, 105, 166
RSA, see Rational Self-Analysis
RSC, see Rational Self-Counseling

Ruhnow, Michael, 222
Ryan, Dr., case history, 17ff; script, 201ff

S

sadness, 25
schools, 217
script, 197ff, 206
secondary alcoholic cravings, 98, 99, 100, 103, 104, 105, 109, 116, 120, 173, 198
self-disclosure in RSC, 114
self-dislike, 24; see also self-image
self-destructive behavior, 82, 216
self-help, 4, 43; see also New Self-Help Treatment
self-image, 18, 24, 99, 100, 112
self-talk, see RSA
semantics, see words
"shall," 162
shame, 25
"should," 160, 162, 166
shyness, 23ff, 77, 95
sleeplessness, 16; and REI, 143
smoke-screens, 184
smoking, 30, 108, 111, 115, 116, 118, 119, 144, 199, 202
snake, see rattlesnake
social drinking, 10, 18, 27, 28, 29, 35, 57, 111, 193, 194, 195, 202, 212
special-breed myth, 185, 186
stage one drinking, 29, 119
stage two drinking, 29, 30, 32, 97
stress, 20, 25, 39, 95, 99, 184, 199
students, 6, 7, 23ff, 95

T

tape recording, 110, 111, 167, 196, 206
telephone therapy, 193
terrorists, 105
therapist, see counselor
thoughts, evaluative, 52, 54, 70, 72, 96; see also ABCs
tobacco, see addiction; see smoking
Training Center for Rational Behavior Therapy and Emotional Self Help, 6, 7, 18, 47, 149, 195
tranquilizers, 30, 51, 216, 217
treatment, see AA; see Intensive Self-Help Alcoholic Treatment Method; see New Self-Help Alcoholic Treatment Method; see medical treatment
"truth" versus "fact", 11, 84

U

V

videotapes, 187ff, 219; see also tape recording

W

"wanting" a drink, 97, 101, 102, 103, 104, 115, 120, 198, 202, 203; see also "craving" versus "wanting;" see also "wishes" and "wants"
weight, 57, 58
Welsh, Richard, 5
"what-if," 184
"wishes" and "wants," 101
withdrawal, 1, 2, 31, 32, 34, 41, 97, 116, 202; drinking from fear of withdrawal, 33; cold turkey, 97, 98, 103; see also medical treatment
words, 21, 47; in beliefs, 64-65, 101, 153, 166, 184. See also specific words and phrases often used irrationally
worry, 25, 73

X

Y

"yes-but," 184
YIPE (Your Irrational Potential Estimate), 183, 224
You and Your Emotions, 218